I don't want any
more cheese

I don't want any more cheese

I just want out of the trap

Richard Templar

London • New York • Toronto • Sydney • Tokyo • Singapore
Hong Kong • Cape Town • Madrid • Paris • Amsterdam • Munich • Milan

PEARSON EDUCATION LIMITED

Head Office:
Edinburgh Gate
Harlow CM20 2JE
Tel: +44 (0)1279 623623
Fax: +44 (0)1279 431059

Website: www.pearsoned.co.uk

First published in Great Britain in 2004

ISBN 0 273 67543 5

British Library Cataloguing in Publication Data
A CIP catalogue record for this book can be obtained from the British Library

10 9 8 7 6 5 4 3 2 1

Typeset by 30
Printed and bound in Great Britain by Bell & Bain Ltd, Glasgow

The Publishers' policy is to use paper manufactured from sustainable forests.

This book is dedicated to Bob Lloyd who longed to escape, dreamed of life outside of the trap… and never quite made it.

Contents

Contents

Part 4 Plans

Last Part Actions

Introduction

All people dream, but not equally. Those who dream by night in the dusty recesses of their mind, wake in the morning to find that it was vanity. But the dreamers of the day are dangerous people, for they dream their dreams with open eyes, and make them come true.

T. E. Lawrence (Lawrence of Arabia)

The best time to work out exactly what you feel about your life, for most of us, is on the journey into work in the morning – on the train or tube, in your car, on your bike or even as you walk. Your mind is relatively fresh and uncluttered by the fog of a day's work and a slight 'just woken up' dopiness helps allow you to answer honestly. So, on your next journey to work, ask yourself:

▶ Do you feel like you're in a trap at work?

▶ Do you long to escape the trap?

▶ Do you want to be free?

▶ Do you dream of something better?

▶ Do you know how to achieve your dream?

If you answered yes to some of these questions, you're certainly not alone. Many of us feel we're in a trap at some point in our lives. We long to escape the trap. We want to be free. We have a plan to get out. In the trap we are mice, accepting cheese as a bribe to keep us there.

But mice like being in mazes; they like cheese, don't they?

We are not mice

Hang on a moment. We're not mice. We are independent, individual, unique, creative people. Yes, we might be in a trap. Yes, we might be accepting cheese because it's easier than following our dream. But deep down inside, if you think you're in a trap, chances are, you're an escapologist who yearns for a new life, a better life, a freer life.

I hate Mondays

So how many more days are you going to sit by the window staring out wishing you were somewhere else, anywhere else? How many more Monday mornings are you going to drag yourself out of bed and off to a job you hate? In an office you resent for a boss you've got no time for? How many more years are you going to squash that dream?

66 How many more Monday mornings
are you going to drag yourself out of bed
and off to a job you hate? 99

So what's holding you back?

▶ Concerned about where the next meal is coming from?

▶ Crap at paperwork?

▶ Fear of failure?

▶ Not enough capital?

▶ Predicting another recession?

▶ Worried about what the family will say?

▶ Don't think your dream is strong enough?

▶ Afraid to cut the ties and go it alone?

▶ Addicted to cheese?

Yes? Yes to some, all or one of these? What holds us in the job is the cheese. It's the promise of a better future, jam tomorrow, safety, security, mindless employment with no fear. Cheese is the glue that binds us to our prison. Cheese is the endless employment with no fun.

So what is cheese? What is the trap?

Cheese is anything that keeps you trapped – the job, the salary, the pension plan, the fear of failure, the responsibility, the duty – it doesn't matter.

The *trap* is the lack of motivation, the drudgery, the sapped will, the job – it doesn't matter.

The trouble with the rat race is that even if you win, you're still a rat.

Lily Tomlin, comedienne

But how do we go about setting ourselves free? Do we get promoted, move to another job, become entrepreneurs, home workers, start our own business, go part-time, become a consultant or a free agent, downshift, work from home, work flexitime, you name it?

"Cheese is the glue that binds us to our prison."

This is not a 'start your own business' book. I'm not going to tell you how to get customers, arrange an overdraft, set up a web site or help you design your letterheads. Nor is this an instruction guide to becoming an entrepreneur. This is the book to help you formulate your dream, do a reality check, make a plan and do it.

This is a book about what makes you tick; what makes you take the cheese, what makes you dream of escape and what's stopped you up until now.

This is a book about what motivates you, what spurs you on, what stimulates you – and what holds you back. This is vital information to include in your escape plan. Now you won't fail. Now you can escape with confidence. Now you can go for it. Run little mouse, run.

Up and out

I only care about getting you up out of the chair and out of your cubicle. I'm only interested in you pursuing your dream. Yep, it might be promotion. It might even be a sideways move to another department. That's fine. I don't want you to quit or walk out or tell the boss where to stuff it (unless that's what you really want and you've

got the 'what next' worked out, of course). I want you to be happy. I want you to want to feel free. And if that means staying in the trap, then good, that's fine. Just so long as you are staying with your eyes open. Just so long as you know what you are doing.

❝ I want you to want to feel free. ❞

There are four easy steps to liberation. First you have to have that dream. Then you have to make a plan of how to achieve it. Then you have to work out how it will affect you and your family and communicate with them about these changes. Then, finally, you have to take some action.

▶ Dream
▶ Plan
▶ Communicate
▶ Act

The reason some of us escape is we do all four. The reason some of us don't is we fail to do any one of the four. Or we may dream but never plan or take action, or we fail to bring the family on board; we fail to communicate properly with them. Perhaps we do dream and communicate and plan and then we never actually do anything – how sad. But there are a lot of us out there who dream and plan and then let it all slide away from us because we can't face uprooting everyone, can't face the possibility that our plan might be rejected. So we suffer in silence. We let those ten years get behind us because no one told us when to run. And sometimes we don't even have a dream. Now that really is sad.

It is better to have ...

You are not going to regret it. You are going to go for it. It might all go wrong. It might not be what you thought. But by golly it will be better to have had a go than not to, and regret that for ever.

This is a book about doing something, anything, to make the dream a reality. Hey, it's your dream. It might be crap. But you'll never sit there one day old and grey and used up and whine that 'if only I could have ...'. I wish I had ...'. The saddest words ever are 'I regret ...'.

66 *This is a book about doing something,*

anything, to make the dream a reality. 99

It was Mike Hanrahan, general manager of Howmett, who first drew my attention to the saying 'I don't want any more cheese; I just want out of the trap'. When he said it, it was one of those light bulb moments. He had been travelling back to the US and had got caught up in some sort of strike – air traffic, baggage handlers, pilots, who knows? who cares? – and had to wait around for a long time. They had offered him coffee, sandwiches, a hotel for the night, a taxi to and from the air terminal to his accommodation, free tickets for some future flights, more coffee and sandwiches. And finally Mike snapped. He went to the desk and just said, 'I don't want any more cheese; I just want out of the trap'.

66 *It was one of those light bulb moments.* 99

Nothing in this world can take the place of persistence. Talent will not; nothing is more common than unsuccessful people with talent.

Genius will not; unrewarded genius is almost a proverb. Education will not; the world is full of educated derelicts. Persistence and determination alone are omnipotent. The slogan 'press on' has solved and always will solve the problems of the human race.

Calvin Coolidge

Sandwich cheese

To him the cheese was, quite literally, cheese. In the sandwiches. But it was all the other offerings. All made to make him accept appalling treatment. All made to get him – and all those other countless, faceless travellers – to be quiet and well behaved.

Cheese is jam tomorrow

I got to thinking about this and saw how many times I had accepted cheese at work. Accepted the offers so I would be quiet, be well behaved, be subservient and malleable. Cheese was future promotions, jam tomorrow, getting on better and higher.

I also realized I didn't enjoy my work particularly but I kept quiet (accepted the cheese) just in case any of these promises might work out. I stayed in the trap accepting cheese because I didn't know there was an alternative. I was scared.

This is a book about bravery. It is a book about refusing cheese so you can enjoy what you are doing more. You might not walk out of the trap, but you can see through the cheese.

Everything in our life is designed to offer us future happiness. At school we are told to work hard so we can pass exams in the future. When we have passed these exams we are told to go on to higher education so we can get a degree or better qualifications. If we get these qualifications we will get a better job. If we get a better job we will earn more money. If we earn more money we will climb the ladder higher and faster.

❝ You can see through the cheese. ❞

If we climb higher and faster we will end up at the top. When we get there we will be rich and thus, of course, happy.

Rabbits in the headlights

Trouble is there are an awful lot of people who get to retirement and look around like rabbits caught in the headlights, searching for their happiness. They have bought the cheese myth for so long that they can't quite believe that for them it didn't bring any happiness after all. They stayed in the trap for forty years unthinkingly accepting cheese.

Cheese has nothing to do with change and everything to do with stagnation and bribery.

Part 1

Cheese, traps and being honest with yourself

'If people are coming to work excited . . . if they're making mistakes freely and fearlessly . . . if they're having fun . . . if they're concentrating on doing things, rather than preparing reports and going to meetings – then somewhere you have leaders.'

Robert Townsend

Being honest with yourself

Ready to escape yet? Not sure? You may need to know just how far down the desperation track you are before you make your move. To do this you have to be totally honest with yourself about:

▶ Your job

▶ How you react to your job

Look, you might be a sales person and find it unbelievably stressful. But Lesley who you work with finds selling fulfils her dream entirely and completely – she is blissfully happy. So what's wrong with you? Is it the job or you? We have to find out.

❝ So what's wrong with you? ❞

I once had a job that initially I found enjoyable. However, the management in their infinite wisdom expanded the job, added bits of responsibility to it and generally changed it until it had the same title but was nothing like the original job. I felt under incredible pressure. I was doing a job I once loved. Was it me or was it the job? In this case it was most definitely the job. I left and went to another company and went back to the original exercise – doing what I loved best: the job. I found that once again I was enjoying myself.

" *Was it me or was it the job?* **"**

Before you go

Before you go it might be worth while checking out the job. Look, if it's the job and you can change the job so that you don't have to shovel down the cheese quite so voraciously, then it might be worth staying. The job may well have been the dream that's turned sour.

> Job dissatisfaction is bad for your health, according to Professor Cary Cooper of the University of Manchester Institute of Science and Technology. His study claims that 30 million working days are lost each year through stress. Dr James Lefanu agrees. Male patients who answered negatively to enquiries about work were often found to be suffering from headaches, palpitations or sleeping difficulties. 'This distress poses a much more significant threat to the physical and mental well-being of young men than virtually everything else combined', he says.

If we can get rid of the stress we might not have to get rid of the job – well, it's worth a try, OK? But how do you tell? How do you decide whether it's the job or you? In a lot of cases it is easy enough. You simply know. But if you don't, then doing the following exercise might be of use. This will tell you where the stress lies and what you have to do about it.

> ❝ *You don't have to shovel down the*
>
> *cheese quite so voraciously.* ❞

Go confidently in the direction of your dreams! Live the life you've imagined. As you simplify your life, the laws of the universe will be simpler; solitude will not be solitude, poverty will not be poverty, nor weakness weakness.

Henry David Thoreau

Before we can deal with what causes you stress at work and give suitable guidelines for what to do about it, we have to be able to identify the sources of the stress. To do this you can fill in the following questionnaire and look up your results afterwards. A similar questionnaire is used by occupational stress management consultants and it has been found to be most beneficial in accurately pin-pointing problem areas at work. This will establish whether it is you or the job. Bear in mind that if you do decide to quit you will still have to do some work afterwards unless you intend being a scrounger for the rest of your life, and I don't believe that of you.

Tick the boxes to the right and score from 0–3	Stress-free 0	Low stress 1	Medium stress 2	High stress 3
1 Not enough work to do				
2 Too much work to do				

Tick the boxes to the right and score from 0–3	Stress-free 0	Low stress 1	Medium stress 2	High stress 3
3 Responsible for others and the way they work				
4 Workplace politics				
5 Changes in work patterns				
6 Too many different roles				
7 Work colleagues				
8 Close friends at work				
9 Remuneration				
10 Environment				
11 Overtime				
12 Taking work home				
13 Working hours – too long or unsociable				
14 Being uncertain as to what is required				
15 Having to make decisions				
16 Deadlines				
17 Boredom				
18 Fear of being dismissed				
19 Training				
20 Under utilised				
21 My relationship with my direct boss				

▶▶

Tick the boxes to the right and score from 0–3	Stress-free 0	Low stress 1	Medium stress 2	High stress 3
22 Thinking about work while away from it				
23 No clear goals to work towards				
24 Conflict at work				
25 Approval, praise and thanks				
26 Job satisfaction				
27 Being promoted too fast/too high				
28 Giving presentations and speaking at meetings				
29 Being closely supervised				
30 Promotion prospects				
31 Support from my partner				
32 Conflict with home				
33 Outside interests conflicting with work				
34 No regular assessments				
35 Outside factors, such as illness or finances, affecting work				
36 Morale of work colleagues				

Each of these statements fits into one of six categories.

- ▶ Home and work
- ▶ Job satisfaction
- ▶ Position
- ▶ Responsibility
- ▶ Work relationships
- ▶ Working pressure

Home and work

This is for questions 12, 22, 31, 32, 33, 35. For a score of over 12 for these six questions you should be thinking more about separating out work from your home life. You need to make sure there are firm boundaries between the two. For a score of between 8 and 12 you still need to separate these two issues a little. For a score of less than 8 you seem to be successfully managing to keep the two apart.

Job satisfaction

This is for questions 9, 10, 18, 20, 26, 30. A score higher than 12 indicates low job satisfaction. You need to look at how highly praised and valued you are, and if not highly enough you need to question whether you are in the right job or working to the right levels of satisfaction. Yep, it's the job alright. For a score of between 8 and 12 you could do with being more satisfied and need to look at this area. For a score of less than 8 you seem to be enjoying work. Maybe you need to look at other areas to find out why you are so dissatisfied.

Position

This is for questions 5, 6, 14, 17, 23, 34. For a score higher than 12 you need to clear up any misunderstandings about your role. What does your job description say? Reaffirm your position with your immediate boss and keep it clearly defined. Look, it's worth a try to keep things sweet. If it doesn't work you can quit afterwards. For a score of between 8 and 12 you still need to be clearer about your position. For a score of less than 8 you have obviously well defined your position and are happy with it.

If you can dream it, you can do it. Always remember this whole thing was started by a mouse.

Walt Disney

Responsibility

This is for questions 3, 4, 15, 24, 28, 29. For a score higher than 12 you seem to be increasingly under pressure with the level of responsibilities you have. Perhaps too much is expected of you or you have been promoted to a post that you are not ready for yet – and perhaps you are unqualified to hold. You should seek retraining or support from your boss. For a score of between 8 and 12 there are problems and you need to look closely at this area. For a score of below 8 you appear to be happy with the level of responsibility you hold.

Work relationships

This is for questions 7, 8, 19, 21, 25, 36. For a score higher than 12 there is obviously severe conflict at work and you need to get immediate support from senior staff to deal with this. For a score of between 8 and 12 there is obvious tension and you need to look at this area closely. For a score of less than 8 you appear to get on well with your work colleagues and find your working environment happy and relatively stress free.

Working pressure

This is for questions 1, 2, 11, 13, 16, 27. A score higher than 12 would indicate you simply have too much work to do. You need to look at delegating or shedding some of your work load. For a score of between 8 and 12 you are still under too much strain and need to look at this area closely. For a score of less than 8 you obviously have enough to do unless you find question 1 a problem, in which case you have too little to do and should seek an increase in your work load or another form of employment. Yep, it could well be the job. Time to run little mouse.

Sorting the wheat from the chaff

There are a lot of issues here to deal with. Quitting when you enjoy the relationships of work, the cut and thrust, but hate the politics or the tedium or whatever, can be rash. You'll find yourself on the outside without support, lonely and unable to function on your own. Perhaps if you have a dream you could modify it to work more with a team. You see what this questionnaire throws up? It highlights problem areas, safe areas and good areas. You have to be able to pick and choose which bits of work are good and which bits are bad. If you could change the bad bits it might be in your best interest to stay. Yes, I know this book is all about saying no to cheese and leaving the trap, but sometimes the trap has to be endured, perhaps for the sake of accumulating some savings or the kids' school fees need paying at the moment and the time isn't right to quit. In which case if you have to stay then it might be worth trying to invest a little time in making the situation better rather than just quitting and solving nothing. Hey, it's your life and you have to do what you have to do. But sometimes we do have a moral responsibility to those around us who depend on us and our wage-earning capabilities. We can't just walk out on them, that would be unforgivable. It is worth looking at what problems would exist even if we did walk out. Are these problems the job or us? If you do run away you will find *you* when you stop running. Is this what you might be running from? Look, changing a few things may remove the trap and have you happy working for cheese again. It may not, but it's worth exploring the possibility.

66 Invest a little time in making

the situation better. 99

Feeling better about work

Here are a few tips about how you might like to handle feeling better about work – you might be here for a while:

▶ **Be assertive.** If you feel under stress, then say so. Express your feelings at work. Don't bottle things up. Be honest with people.

▶ **Be clear about what is work and what is not.** Separate your work from your home life. Don't take work home with you – and don't take your home problems to work with you.

▶ **Be comfortable.** Make sure your working environment is warm enough/cool enough. Have whatever you need to be comfortable enough to get the job done properly, but not so comfortable that you fall asleep.

▶ **Be committed.** If you have chosen to do the job, then get on with it. If you find you can't, then quit the trap.

▶ **Be focused at work.** You are there to do a task, so do it. You are not there to muck about, flirt with staff, enjoy the free coffee, the company car or the paid holidays. You're there to do a job – do it.

When rats leave a sinking ship, where exactly do they think they're going?

Douglas Gauck

▶ **Be healthy.** Make sure the job is adding to your health and not detracting from it. This applies to your moral and emotional health just as much as your physical health. If the job you are doing goes against the grain of your personal views and beliefs, you will suffer stress.

▶ **Be organized.** Plan your work load, your desk, your diary, your day. Don't put things off, do things when you are supposed to and don't delay tasks.

▶ **Don't take on too much.** You aren't superhuman. If you have junior staff, use them. Delegate. Learn to say no to too much work.

▶ **Eat sensibly.** You should gear your food intake to the type of work you have to do. If you are a manual worker, you need more calories. If your important meetings are in the afternoon, don't have a heavy alcoholic lunch. Don't binge on high-calorie snacks. Watch your intake of coffee and other caffeine drinks. Don't smoke. Be aware of your drinking habits and patterns.

❝ *Go home when you are supposed to.* ❞

▶ **Have a fixed working day – and stick to it.** Go home when you are supposed to. If you say you're going to stop at a certain time, make sure you do. Try to get the home/work balance right.

▶ **Have a life.** Make sure you don't spend all your time working, thinking about work, talking about work.

Have some friends who don't work in the same business. Have hobbies and social activities that take you away from your work areas.

▶ **Have goals.** Make sure the job you are doing furthers your personal life goals and that you aren't just filling in time waiting for something better to turn up. Make plans to make sure it does turn up if that is the case. Remember your dream and turn to the next section to start making plans to achieve it.

▶ **Take breaks.** You need to get away from work every now and again. This might be every few hours, days, weeks or months, but no one should expect you to work without suitable and beneficial breaks.

▶ **Work to live, not the other way round.** When all is said and done it's only a job. It might be very important to you, but your health, happiness and welfare come first.

▶ **You are entitled to support.** If you need to retrain, develop new skills, improve, get help or even just talk about work problems, you should be able to enlist support from the senior staff above you. You might stay in the trap, but you might be a lot happier.

In this rat race everybody's guilty till proved innocent!

Bette Davis

Stress and work, work and stress

A lot of this spotlights stress. Are you stressed? Is it the job or is it you? How bad is that stress? Will you go mad if you don't quit? Should you be seriously thinking of medical intervention you are so close to breaking point? Let's have a look at what happens when we get really stressed by our work – bearing in mind you still have to work after escaping from the trap. This is the sort of thing you should be looking out for. Display more than about three of these symptoms and you need to think seriously about quitting the trap.

▶ Accident proneness

▶ Aggressive behaviour

▶ Anxiety

▶ Apathy

▶ Avoidance of confrontation

▶ Depression

▶ Difficulty making decisions

▶ Difficulty sleeping

▶ Difficulty thinking

- ▶ Drug taking
- ▶ Early waking
- ▶ Emotional instability
- ▶ Excessive alcohol consumption
- ▶ Excessive smoking
- ▶ Fatigue and exhaustion
- ▶ Inactivity
- ▶ Insomnia
- ▶ Listlessness
- ▶ Negative emotional responses – guilt, shame, loneliness, jealousy, moodiness
- ▶ Negative self-awareness

- Nervousness
- Overeating/loss of appetite
- Panic attacks
- Permanent numbness
- Phobias
- Tension
- Trembling

If you are suffering from several of these – maybe one or two are fairly natural to us all – then you really do need to be communicating about how you feel being in the trap.

It is not necessary to change. Survival is not mandatory.
W. Edwards Deming

Staying in the trap causes illness

Staying in the trap causes stress. Don't have nightmares, but the stress caused by being in the wrong job, working under the wrong sort of pressure, can cause serious illness. Stress is a bad thing when it affects your health. If you're a racing driver then stress – and unbelievable stress – is part and parcel of your job; and it's stress you love or you wouldn't be a racing driver. Sitting in a dull office doing something you hate all day produces a different sort of stress and one that is much more damaging. So switch now from driving a desk to racing cars, or whatever else your dream happens to be.

66 Sitting in a dull office doing something you hate all day produces a different sort of stress. 99

Accepting cheese

Sometimes, when perhaps we are younger, we accept cheese without thinking. We are happy to accept all the lies, all the myths, and we are determined to 'get to the top' no matter what. We don't stop to think about the reality of what we are doing or the long-term implications or what it might be doing to our health or even the karmic effect. By this I mean the effect of what we are doing on our psyche – Robert Maxwell had to live with himself, he too had to look in the mirror every morning. We all have a conscience to live with. We all have ourselves to answer to about what we do for a living. And there are times when we all lie to ourselves about:

▶ The environmental damage that is caused by what we do for a living

▶ What damage is being done to our health by what we do for a living

▶ How true to ourselves we are being

Now I'm not saying we're in the same league as Maxwell, no way near it. Or at least I do hope not.

❝ Robert Maxwell had to live with himself. ❞

So, we once had a dream. Now we are bored, listless, fed up, dreaming again of following our true self and doing what we once wanted to instead of doing what we know we don't want to. We are fed up with cheese and long to escape the trap. But escaping seems so daunting, so final, so scary, so risky, so downright dangerous. Isn't it better, safer, warmer to stay and accept the cheese? Isn't it the done thing to live off cheese?

66 *Escaping seems so daunting.* **99**

If you can dream it, you can do it.

Walt Disney

It's an option, one option. It is entirely up to you. You can stay or go. If you stay you know that you are accepting the cheese and that's fine. You may wish to consider the cheese. Ask for better cheese. Move to another part of the trap and have slightly different cheese. You may like to move to a new trap altogether and have entirely foreign cheese.

Or you may like to escape

Escaping is dangerous. Escaping is risky. It might be the riskiest thing you've ever done. You may feel cold and scared and threatened. But you will feel alive. Following your dream also involves other people – your partner, your children, your friends – and you can't operate in isolation. What you do has an effect and in a later section we will deal with how you make that effect positive and inclusive rather than negative and exclusive. In your dream you may see yourself already there, already achieving whatever it is you want to do. But there are a lot of steps to go yet.

❝ *It might be the riskiest thing you've ever done.* ❞

part 2

Dreams

To fulfil a dream, to be allowed to sweat over lonely labour, to be given a chance to create, is the meat and potatoes of life. The money is the gravy.

Bette Davis

What are you going to do?

What do you *think* you are going to do? What do you really, really want to do? What is your dream? How do you *think* you could go about realising that dream? Could changing jobs fill that void? Or must you get out of your industry altogether? Can you take early retirement? Cash in your pension? How about voluntary redundancy? This is the planning section. This is writing the escape plan. You don't do anything in this section but you do have to be realistic. This is a section looking at the possible options – stay, get out, do what once you do get out?

Stop the mindless wishing that things would be different. Rather than wasting time and emotional and spiritual energy in explaining why we don't have what we want, we can start to pursue other ways to get it.

Greg Anderson, US basketball player

So where is out of the trap?

Out is anything you want it to be – your own business, working from home, downshifting, moving to another job, promotion, starting your own consultancy, becoming a free agent, working part-time, starting a family, working flexitime, going round the world, giving it all up to work for a good cause. This section is about:

▶ Identifying the cheese and finding ways to replace it. What are you going to do instead? What's your dream?

▶ Identifying the trap and seeing a way out. How are you going to do it?

▶ Making sure everyone else is on board with your dream. Are you emotionally ready for escape?

▶ Identifying the out and getting there. Taking the first/next step

This isn't a book for mice.

So you need to ask yourself a whole series of questions:

▶ What is my dream?

▶ What was my dream when I was a kid?

▶ How realistic do I think my dream is?

▶ What stopped me fulfilling this dream right from the word go?

▶ What distracted me?

▶ What cheese am I accepting now?

▶ How do I think I can achieve my dream?

At this stage you don't have to do anything except be honest with yourself. If you don't have a dream, then fine. You can put this book away until you do have one. You don't have to have a dream. You mustn't feel that just because everyone else has dreams, you have to have them too. If you are happy with the cheese, then fine. If you want more cheese, then that's fine too. There is no judgement in any of this. There is no right or wrong, no better or worse. Some of us want out and some of us don't. That's all fine too.

❝ You don't have to do anything except

be honest with yourself. ❞

So what if I don't have a dream?

Then go back to the beginning and get a dream and come back. No, seriously, if you don't have a specific dream, that's OK. We can work with what you *feel* you want to do, rather than *knowing* what you want to do. The mistake some make is walking out without having a clue what they feel they want to do. You have to have some basic direction to go in or you'll wander aimlessly for ever. And what if you really can't stand it any longer but don't have a direction? Then walking may give you the impetus to make up your mind, but somehow I doubt it. Perhaps better to stay put and spend some time working with what you think you want. Is it:

▶ A change of scenery?
▶ A new job title?
▶ A new job?
▶ Moving to a new department?
▶ More challenges?
▶ Out of the trap altogether?
▶ Your own business?

▶ A new lifestyle?

▶ A new location?

Come on, some of these must ring bells. I thought so. It's only a question of asking the right questions. And let's face it, you wouldn't be reading this if you didn't have an inkling, would you?

What if you are already living the dream and are still sick of cheese?

If this is the case with you then I think you have to:

▶ Reconsider your dream
▶ Reconsider the cheese

Look, life isn't perfect. It never will be. Take myself. When I was a kid, and I mean really young, maybe six, I had a dream. I was going to be a writer. I was going to have six children. I was going to live in a big house in the country. I was going to be married to a French girl. My sister wanted to be an actress and come down to visit all her nephews and nieces in a bright red sports car and wearing a big floppy hat. She was an actress for a while but eventually abandoned the cheese and the trap and now works with the homeless in London. She doesn't have a red sports car or a big floppy hat; she comes down to visit on the train. For some, being an actress might have been their dream, but for her it was a trap. She was only really doing it because it was expected of her because all of our older brothers had gone 'on the stage'.

Dare to live the life you have dreamed for yourself. Go forward and make your dreams come true.

Ralph Waldo Emerson

My dream didn't happen for over forty years. Yes, I had the six children. Yes, I had the big house in the country. Yes, I am married to a French girl.[1] But the writing side didn't materialise for forty years. I got my first book published when I was forty-six. It's a long wait. In the meantime I had a 'career'. I ate cheese big time. I spent many years loving the trap, enjoying the cheese. But at the back of my mind there was always the niggling little voice: 'When are you going to be real? When are you going to be true to yourself? When are you going to throw away that suit and write your book? When, when, when?'

❝ I ate cheese big time. ❞

I managed not to listen. Sure, I wanted to write. Sure, I wanted to follow my dream. But I also thought I had to earn a living. I had to feed kids, pay a mortgage, put bread on the table. It took a whole series of catastrophes for me to be forced to act; forced to start to live out my dream. I got a sort of cosmic kick up the arse.

❝ I got a sort of cosmic kick up the arse. ❞

Now I live my dream. But, as I was saying a while back, life ain't perfect. I still have deadlines.

---

[1] Well, she's actually Portuguese but it was always my sister who said 'French'; in my dream all I specified was 'beautiful, dark hair, tall, foreign'.

I love deadlines. I love the whooshing sound they make as they fly by.

Douglas Adams, writer

I still have to chase work. There are some mornings when I simply can't face writing another bloody word. I have lean times when there isn't enough money. I have bad days when publishers give me the run-around and I could happily kill them. There are bad times.

The dream is real, my friends. The failure to realize it is the only reality.

Toni Cade Bambara (1939–1995), US writer

Yes, I am living my dream and I'm sure there are many who would envy that if they too wanted to write. But at no point do I say 'I don't want any more cheese, I just want out of the trap'. I don't feel I'm in a trap because, mostly, I have control. And that is the big difference. When I have those bad days when I can't face sitting at this desk, I can go and sit in the sunshine or take the dogs for a walk or go back to bed. I can sit here and write, dressed in an old dressing gown, at four in the morning. I set my own agenda. If there is any cheese going, it is self-made cheese. If this is a trap, then I hold the keys. But living your dream can be hard work. It can require guts and determination and incredible reserves of drive.

❝ If there is any cheese going, it is

self-made cheese. ❞

I guess the way you tell whether you are living your dream is to imagine yourself doing anything else. I can't.

Well, maybe a small boatyard on a Greek island, but that's more a fantasy than a dream. We'll talk about the reality of your dream in a bit. So would I change? No. Is this a trap? Sometimes, but as I said, I hold the keys. Can I see myself doing something else? No, not really, never. Is there cheese? Depends on how hard I work. Sometimes there's only bread and sometimes the very best stilton money can buy.

To be honest I don't think you can live the dream and be sick of cheese; it's an either–or situation. Living the dream means you've rejected someone else's cheese for your dream. Their cheese is your dream sat on. Once you reject their cheese, your dream can happen. Once your dream comes alive, their cheese is redundant. You have to see the cheese as a bribe to keep you pacified. Once you see that, the bribe doesn't work any more.

66 Living the dream means you've rejected
someone else's cheese for your dream. 99

How do you tell when it's time to get out?

You'll know. There will come a point when getting out will be either thrust upon you from on high or you'll simply walk. Or you'll be so stressed you'll have to do something. But whatever, you'll know. Sometimes the dream just has to burst out. Sometimes it bursts in. What do I mean by that? Apparently we can learn a lot about the state of our inner self by watching what we dream about at night when we are asleep. In a recent survey nearly 60 per cent of UK employees said they regularly wake up in a cold sweat.[2] And those cold sweats are caused by work-related nightmares. More than half of those nightmares are caused by stress. Here are the figures:

- ▶ 10 per cent have bad dreams about getting laid off
- ▶ 41 per cent sleep badly because they can't stop worrying about work
- ▶ 23 per cent lose sleep because they feel they are in a career rut

[2] A poll of more than 1,000 workers by online-learning specialist Learndirect.

- 20 per cent just lie there unable to sleep because they feel inadequate at work
- 25 per cent of the nightmares occur on a Sunday night
- Most nightmares occur during busy work periods
- 25 per cent say they dream about work in a negative way at least once a week

❝ 25 per cent of the nightmares occur on a Sunday night. ❞

Interesting? I think so. So what form do these nightmares take?

- Arguing with the boss
- Being late for an important meeting
- Lusting after a colleague
- Having to give an unexpected presentation
- Going to work naked
- The computer crashing
- Wanting to kill the boss

You'll know. As I say, sometimes the dream just bursts out. Sometimes you just can't take no more cheese.

Education vs relocation

And when that 'no more cheese' moment comes, what are you going to do? There is an old saying for dealing with dodgy relationships; there are always only three options when things are going badly:

▶ Put up with it

▶ Change it

▶ Dump it

If you've reached the 'no more cheese' time then obviously you can't put up with it. So that leaves only two options – change it or dump it. For this we call these two options *education* and *relocation*.

Education is where you learn how to cope by changing your situation within your organization – moving sideways, getting promoted out of your rut, changing departments, rekindling the challenge of your career, changing what you actually do but not leaving. Relocation is obvious – relocating you to another career entirely or to another part of the country. We'll deal with where you are going to go later on – and what to do if you want to stay.

❝ If you've reached the 'no more cheese' time then obviously you can't put up with it. ❞

What do you want to *do* when you grow up? What do you want to *be* when you grow up?

In my dream when I was a kid I wanted to *be* a writer. *Being* a writer was an all-embracing, total thing. I wasn't *doing* writing, I was *being* a writer. It's an interesting distinction to tell whether you are following your heart or chasing a pay packet. What do you *do* for a living? Do you *do* it or *be* it? When I wasn't a writer I earned a living for a long time as a finance manager. I never wanted to *be* a finance manager; it became something I did. The silly thing was that throughout my entire adult life my passport always said 'writer' under occupation. This was a tiny private dream fulfilment wish thing that I did, a sort of small rebellion against having to earn a living doing something I never really felt at home doing.

Do you walk tall?

I am a writer. What are you? Are you proud of what you are? Does it make you walk taller? When someone asks

what you do or what you are, do you reply easily? Or haltingly? Reluctantly? Joyfully or sadly?

Look, it might be that you are quite happy doing what you do, happy living on a diet of cheese, happy being you. That's fine. So what are you reading this for? Yep, thought so. You wouldn't be reading this if there wasn't a need to say no to cheese, a need to change, a need to fulfil a dream.

❝ Are you proud of what you are? ❞

The creative approach to the no-cheese diet

Saying no to cheese is all very well but you have to have something to replace it. It's no good wandering around saying, 'I've got to get out or I'll go mad'. You have to have an escape plan. You have to have a dream. You have to have a goal, a focus, a vision. This is the reality. You have to be able to set your eyes to some distant horizon that has a certainty to it. It's no good shilly-shallying. You have to leap with both eyes open and know exactly where you are going. You have to come to the edge and you have to jump. No one is going to push you. No one is going to bribe you to jump. No one is going to tell you to jump. This is about you. This is about knowing where it is you are jumping to.

And if you don't know, then you have to create your dream. You have to be very realistic about your talents, your strengths, your interests. You have to know what drives you, what motivates you.

We'll deal later with all the things you can do to make your dream take shape and how to test it for leaks. You are going to have to start thinking sideways, looking for opportunities, thinking outside of the box. No, really. Up to now you may well have been thinking outside of the box for your job, but you have to go beyond that and think outside of your thinking outside of the box. Now you have to be prepared to adopt a totally flexible approach to your dream and fulfilling it.

Accepting cheese means you have learnt to be quiet, subservient, normal, acceptable, good, nice, obedient, formal, submissive, respectful, docile, deferential.

Now you are going to break out and be original, lateral, spontaneous, creative, impulsive, quick, in control, in charge, decisive, assertive, determined, demanding.

Before you walked; now you are going to fly.

Marketing yourself

Once you have a dream, once you have a plan, you also have a product – you. You are your own brand and as such you are going to have to stand out from the crowd. You are going to have to market your product. No longer can you hide anonymously behind some grey, faceless organization. You are going to have to step into the spotlight and be centre stage. You are going to have to market yourself. You are going to have to sell you.

❝ Before you walked; now you are going to fly. ❞

Celebrate – you've just been made redundant/ sacked/laid off

Sometimes we need the cosmic kick up the arse. Being made redundant can be a disaster or a kick up the backside. Which do you want it to be? Can you see it as a ticket to freedom or a route to despair? The brilliant thing is, it is entirely up to you. You can be angry, feel rejected, curse and scream, feel hurt, cry, swear, threaten them with legal action. Or quietly walk away whistling. Sshhh. It's your choice, but don't let on.

Basically they've just cut off your cheese rations and you ought to be bloody grateful. Bet it came as a shock. Bet you felt cheated, let down, angry. I know what it is like. I was demoted once during a major takeover. It felt shit. What did I do? Why, failed to seize the opportunity and hung on in there. Worked and wormed and worried my way back up. Admittedly, once I got back up in the saddle again I looked around and saw that being up here wasn't as fab as I had once thought. The gingerbread had lost some of its gilt and I resolved to escape as soon as possible. And yep, I too went through all the stuff you'll go through – What about that regular pay packet? What will my family say? Where will I go and what will I do? Yep, I too had all those questions and the answers somehow came, were worked out.

❝ Where will I go and what will I do?❞

Depression and the inability to do anything

If you really are in the trap, deep in the doldrums, it can be extremely difficult to rouse yourself to do anything, let alone escape. We'll look at the symptoms of stress a little later on, but if you find yourself sitting with your head in your hands too often and have no ability to think clearly about escaping, you may need professional help to get out or even to stay in.

Ageing and escaping

There is also something to do with age that can make us slip into apathy. Shame that, as when we are young we are much more likely to take the cheese and ask no questions. As we get older we are less likely to swallow the company lies and want to get out, tick tock, tick tock, the clock is measuring out our life, and as we get older panic sets in and we realize that if we don't do something now we might never do it. But in that panic comes paralysis and we can't move, frozen to the spot with fear of failure.

> *Tick tock, tick tock, the clock is measuring out our life.*

A lot of people begin to question more as they approach forty – hence mid-life crisis. We also question more at our quarter-life crisis; this occurs around twenty-eight and causes many changes. If we haven't been married, we'll suddenly get married. If we've been childless, we'll suddenly start a family. If we've travelled a lot, we'll suddenly settle down.

We, apparently, also question more in January – turning over a new leaf and New Year's resolutions, that sort of thing. We also question more on a Monday morning.

What do we spend our time on?

We spend about 2,000 hours a year working. That's a lot. That's a life sentence. That's not work, that's drudgery, slavery. After some twenty years of this – 40,000 hours – we are ready to blow. We explode, and no wonder. All those hours spent working for someone else, making someone else wealthy, pushing bits of paper around someone else's desk (oh, you think it's your desk do you? Try taking it home with you and you'll find out whose it is). We get to thirty or thirty-five or forty and just explode, walk out the door, have an affair, buy a silly red sports car, take a hike, tell the boss to stuff it and leave. Whoa there. Blow out that fuse and let's take a little time to think this through before the dynamite moment. Take a moment to plan where you want to be and where you are now and see whether it isn't a simple case of joining the dots without the fireworks.

Getting older

There's also something about getting older that means the pay rises don't come so fast, we don't get offered quite so many new challenges, young blood gets pro-moted over us. Thus we get more despondent and start looking for the exit signs. Young bloods invariably have more time to stay abreast of developments. They are also hungrier, leaner, meaner, keener to make their mark. They too will learn it ain't all sweet-smelling cheese.

66 *It ain't all sweet-smelling cheese.* **99**

Also, whatever industry we work in, things change faster and faster. We don't though. We get slower and slower. As our industry gets more modern, we feel less in touch with innovations and start to feel things are getting slightly out of control. The thought of staying where we are for another twenty years or so starts to look less attractive. But we are still sharp. We are still young. We are still up for it. Yes, we are. But we may have grown stale and need a new challenge to get that old adrenaline flowing again. Time to go.

Unless of course you have retained the vision, the focus, the goal. But then if you have you'll be happy to stay right where you are, and I don't believe you want that or you wouldn't be reading this.

66 *The thought of staying where we are for*

another twenty years or so starts

to look less attractive. **99**

Types of dreams

A quick note before we press on with helping you escape. If you have a dream, spend a moment or two considering how realistic it is. For instance, I once had a dream of sailing single-handed around the world. Yes, seriously. No, don't laugh. It was my dream. However, it wasn't really realistic for several reasons. I don't like sailing. What I wanted to do was motor boat around the world, but that ain't so easy – can't carry that much fuel. Also, I didn't do it when I was young. Now I have small children etc and commitments etc I simply couldn't go without abandoning everyone, which I am not prepared to do. Thus I have compromised my dream and spend happy warm days motor boating on the local river. Oh yes, another reason, I have no sense of direction – I'd have got lost before leaving Falmouth.

> *If you have a dream, spend a moment or two considering how realistic it is.*

You might have to modify your dream for many reasons:

▶ Age (you might want to join the army/navy/airforce at sixty-three but if they stop taking 'em when they reach twenty-eight, you aren't going to get in. You'll have to adapt, modify, compromise – join the TA, buy your own boat, learn to fly a light aircraft)

- ▶ Commitments (children, cats, ageing parents, that sort of thing. We couldn't countenance irresponsible behaviour. Sort out your commitments before you escape, not after)

- ▶ Lack of ability (I did dream of being a water colour painter for many years but eventually had to accept my talents were definitely not in that direction. However, I did have fun finding out and making a wonderful mess)

- ▶ Fitness (dreaming of romping across the Australian bush when you're ninety-two and arthritic may need a little modification – but I did know someone who did this, so don't go giving up)

Kill my boss? Do I dare live out the American dream?

Homer Simpson

Now I'm not saying don't do it. I'm not saying you can't do it. All I'm suggesting is a little bit of being realistic before you embark on a new career or lifestyle will help you make the dream come true and not be a disappointment.

The point of a dream

Now we shall assume you have a dream.[3] We shall assume it is realistic, attainable and will satisfy. Now, you

---

[3] I'm not sure what you do if you don't have a dream. Get one I guess. How you go about doing that is up to you. I'm not copping out here, merely being realistic. Having a dream has always been a central part of my life and I can't conceive of not having one. But I am prepared to accept that there may be people out there who don't have one but still want out of the trap. I guess you will have to do some pretty deep soul searching to see what you are good at, where you might be happiest – or even happier – what you are good at. There are a lot of career consultants only too anxious to offer their services.

have to find out what the point of your plan is. For instance, you might want to start your own smallholding. Fine, but what is the actual point of that? You might say, 'I've always wanted to be a smallholder, a farmer'. Fine, but what's the point? For instance:

▶ To be self-sufficient

▶ To lead a healthier life

▶ To be closer to a rural community

▶ To raise animals and find out more about husbandry

▶ To live organically

There may be loads more, hey, I'm not the one who wants to be a smallholder. There has to be a point. Once you identify the point you can move on to making plans to achieve it. If you want to speak in business speak, the point of your dream is the setting of your objective – what exactly it is you seek to achieve, how you measure your success. Just saying 'a smallholder' isn't an objective. Let's suppose your objective, your point in being a smallholder, is to raise animals to help feed people and to live more healthily. Once you've established this you can begin to look around and see that having a point opens up your options. Being a smallholder isn't the only way to achieve your objective. You might well be able to raise animals to help feed people in other circumstances rather than just moving to the countryside and buying a small-holding which may well be someone else's failed dream. (And it may well have failed because they didn't know their objective, their point.)

We've removed the ceiling above our dreams. There are no more impossible dreams.

Jesse Jackson

Maybe the smallholding isn't a good example. Let's say you want to chuck it all in and be a water colour painter. Now ask why. Why do I want this dream?

▶ To impress the world with my talent

▶ To discover new techniques

▶ To explore my creativity

▶ To exhibit in galleries

▶ To push the medium to its limit

▶ To collaborate with other painters

▶ To swan about looking cool in a smock (and Dalí moustache for the men amongst us)

▶ To move to Italy where the light is better and painting is actually a bit of an excuse, I'm really going for the wine

See? There is now a whole range of options opening up.

Write down what it is you want to achieve. Write down why you want to do this – what's the point. This is your objective. By this you can judge whether you have succeeded or failed. Be very clear about the point of your dream, the long-term goal, what it is you expect to get out of it.

Look, I hate doing this as much as you do but it has to be done. If I suggest to a publisher a book title, they will ask, 'what's it for?' I then have to justify it, sell it to them. You have no one – except perhaps family – to sell your idea to, but you have to be very clear about it or you risk failing. You almost need to write yourself a proposal – position, problem, possibilities, proposal:

▶ Position – I am stuck in this dead-end job

▶ Problem – I am slowly losing my marbles, I phone in sick too often and have been known to burst into tears on a Sunday night just thinking about coming in to work on a Monday

▶ Possibilities – I stay here and go bananas, I kill the boss and go to prison, I follow my heart and open my own business, I look for another job that I don't really want

▶ Proposal – I start my own business

Now sell it to yourself:

I want to start my own business making children's rocking horses. I have done this as a hobby for the last twenty years and have sold several to friends and family. I have made contact with a leading toy store chain and they say they can shift up to twenty a year. I love making them and feel happy working with wood. My point is to be a master craftsperson, skilled in what I do, taking pleasure and satisfaction in creating something that will last and bring great pleasure to small children and reinforce a more natural, less technological childhood for them. My objective is to be self-employed doing something I love and selling what I make to provide a decent income for me and my family.

Good.

So, shall we get on with making plans for making your dream come true?

❝ *I stay here and go bananas, I kill the boss*

and go to prison. **❞**

Oh, by the way you won't find any 'what we learnt in this chapter' bits in this book. Nor will you find many case studies. I always think that if they don't talk directly to you about your own personal experience, you'll switch off and stop reading. So I'm talking to you about your dream, your plan, your escape, not to you about someone else's. On we go.

part 3

Communication

It is one of the strange ironies of this strange life [that] those who work the hardest, who subject themselves to the strictest discipline, who give up certain pleasurable things in order to achieve a goal, are the happiest people.

Brutus Hamilton

How will you make it happen?

In this section we shall look at the emotional side of escape. Have you talked to your partner yet about your dream? The kids? How will it affect everyone around you? Do you have their support yet? How will it affect you? Are you emotionally ready to go off and work for yourself or run a B&B in the country or whatever else it might be that is your dream? How will the dream match up to the reality? What happens if you discover you have made a mistake? Can you go back into the trap? Would you want to?

In this section you don't have to do anything really except talk to people, gather advice, make some notes, make plans, look out of the trap and begin to smell the coffee.

❝ *Look out of the trap and begin to*

smell the coffee. **❞**

Talking to yourself

Before you can talk to your loved ones about your dream, you have to have an 'inner dialogue'. Sorry to go all New

Age on you but it is true. You have to talk to yourself thoroughly and completely before you can talk to others. You have to know exactly why you have to go before you can escape and take others with you. You may be embarking on a long and dangerous road and they will want to know you have thought things through pretty thoroughly before joining you.

Now, we'll assume you've had this inner dialogue and are ready to sell this dream to your partner and children if you have them.

> ❝ They will want to know you have thought
> things through pretty thoroughly. ❞

Being honest with others around you

If you are unhappy with your life, it is your right to say so. That's it. It is your right. You don't have to put up or shut up. You don't have to bottle it all up. You don't have to suffer in silence. If you have suffered so long in silence it can be difficult to suddenly announce you have had enough and want to throw caution to the wind, move to the Outer Hebrides and start a sheep farm (or whatever they do in the Outer Hebrides and frankly I don't want you to write in to tell me, it could be seaweed farming for all I care, others are free to follow their dream and if it involves cold rocky islands then that is their business, not mine).

> ❝ You don't have to bottle it all up. You don't
> have to suffer in silence. ❞

So how are you going to do it? If you can't blurt it all out in one splurge, what can you do? Simple answer is ask for help. Admitting that you are unhappy is one thing, announcing a complete new lifestyle in the same breath ain't. You have to take it bit by bit. Outline the position first. Look, this is easy stuff. You do it all day at work – position, problem, possibilities, proposal.

- ▶ The position is that I am unhappy in my job
- ▶ The problem is I've had enough cheese
- ▶ The possibilities are:
  1 that I could continue but go mad,
  2 that I could leave and follow my dream which, as you know, is to be a ....
- ▶ The proposal is that we talk about this and try to find a solution

Then add, 'what do you think?'

If you are selling a radical change of lifestyle, pace, location, work ethic, dream or whatever, then it is only fair that you allow everyone else to have their say. It would be rare indeed to hear:

'Yes, I know you're sick of it but you really have no choice. I suggest you just try to knuckle down and give up these silly ideas of yours to become a ...... and get your head down and get on with your work. It's not my problem that you are unhappy and are cracking up. We need the money coming in and you'd better just pull yourself together and shape up.'

Yuck. I say rare, but not impossible. Have a fall-back position if indeed you do hear anything like that. Before you do though, just do a quick reality check:

▶ Am I always suggesting harebrained schemes?

▶ Is this another one of them?

▶ Have I run up amazing amounts of debt that it would be unrealistic to walk away from?

▶ Have we recently gone through a major life change and would it be unfair to thrust another one on anyone at this time?

▶ Have we recently gone through a major stress event such as the death of a close relative or children leaving home (or getting arrested or being in other trouble), a birth or a major illness and would it be unrealistic to add to the stress at this time?

▶ Is this the first time I have ever mentioned this and thus it is a complete shock and might take some adjustment?

▶ Is the dream of mine in direct competition to that of my partner?

▶ Is my dream attainable and thus worth pursuing or totally unrealistic and thus not likely to happen? (For an example I have a friend who is fairly insistent that he is going to be a famous singer one day; the fact that he is tone deaf, sings flat and is totally unmusical doesn't seem to have impinged on him one iota. He is in desperate need of a reality check)

▶ Am I in the throws of a nervous breakdown and anything I say should be treated with considerable caution? (Not impossible)

▶ Is this in fact a mask for something else totally unconnected, ie I have been having an affair with my boss and it is now over and I want to put as much space between us as possible and this seems like a good way of running away?

▶ Am I in fact just running away anyway?

OK, the reality check's over – and there may be other things you can think of. We shall assume you and your dream are all true and real and for the finest of reasons. Now you have to sell it. You have to persuade your partner that it will be good for them too. I guess you're going to have to do this – I don't know your dream well enough, or your partner come to that.

❝Am I always suggesting harebrained schemes?❞

Being honest about your dream

You may think it's fab. You may be convinced it's the bestest dream that there's ever been in the whole history of the universe. You may not want to hear a word against it – but …Yes, there's always a but. This is it. But your partner doesn't have a pair of your rose-tinted specs and will see all the flaws, loopholes, hurdles, drawbacks, errors, imperfections and shortcomings in your precious dream. And they are going to point them out to you.

Before you go outlining paradise, it is worth doing another reality check on the dream itself:

▶ Have you sounded this out on someone independent whose advice you value and who won't pull their punches with you?

▶ Have you sought legal, professional and practical advice from those in the know – your solicitor, accountant, bank manager, boss (you'll need to know how much notice to give, what your pension rights are, etc), someone who works in your intended new business?

▶ Can you afford it?

- Is it attainable? (Yes, this one again)
- Is it you?
- Is there a real role for your partner so that they don't become excess baggage or ballast (or in the worst case a millstone)?
- Have you thought this through?
- Have you written a plan complete with financial and emotional costings?
- Have you taken everyone else into consideration? Kids? Parents? Pets?
- Have you considered the long-term ramifications? Pensions? Retirement? Illness? Old age?

Then, once you present all this evidence of how carefully you've thought it all through, you'll find your partner will highlight the one area you missed, the one flaw you've failed to spot. They aren't being picky, just careful. It's their future as well you know. Now you're down to discussing, negotiating, working out the fine details. Haggling if you like.

Being honest about your ability to turn your dream into a reality

Your dream may be fab. You may be fab. But can you turn this dream into reality? How well do you know you? Your partner may need some persuading. Before you present your plan, your dream, it might be worth checking *your* compatibility with your dream. For instance, you may feel you want to be a cruise ship entertainer (look, it does happen, this is someone's dream, so stop laughing), perhaps a stand-up comic. But you've never appeared in public before. How good are you going to be at it? What do you think? Let's have a look.

❝ It does happen, this is someone's dream,

so stop laughing. ❞

Yes, everybody's dying to be someone else, but I'll live my life if it kills me.

e. e. cummings

Compatibility tests

A lot of work unhappiness is caused by trying to force yourself into a round hole – you being a square peg. It has happened to me many times and the only thing to do is quit and start again somewhere else doing something else. That's where these tests come in useful – they help you identify the shape of your particular peg – round, square, triangular, irregular, etc.

There are various types of tests – I guess you have to find the one which suits you – and the best known are the Myers Briggs type, the Keirsey Temperament Sorter and the Enneagram (which always sounds like a microscopic amount of food for people on diets or a cross between an enigma and an anagram). What they all do is classify the population into various types – helper, leader, enthusiast, achiever, perfectionist, peacemaker, that sort of thing. The number of personality types varies from test to test, from four (the Keirsey Temperament Sorter) through nine (Enneagram) to sixteen (Myers Briggs).[4]

---

[4] If you want to find any of these, do a simple search on the internet and you'll turn up enough sites to keep you busy.

Nobody motivates today's workers. If it doesn't come from within, it doesn't come. Fun helps remove the barriers that allow people to motivate themselves.

Herman Cain

Look at this list and tell me which word resonates with you, makes you notice it, makes you think it might have something to do with you:

1 Assertive

2 Possessive

3 Communicator

4 Protective

5 Creative

6 Critic

7 Harmonious

8 Intensive

9 Free

10 Prudent

11 Independent

12 Emotional

Now look at this list:

1 Perfectionist

2 Helper

3 Achiever

4 Individualist

5 Observer

6 Team-player

7 Enthusiast

8 Leader

9 Peacemaker

Or how about:

1 Artist

2 Rationalist

3 Guardian

4 Idealist

The second one is from the Enneagram testing. The third one is from the Keirsey Temperament Sorter. The first one? Oh, the first one. That is traditional, old-fashioned astrology. Look, I didn't say I believed in any of this, just that it is a good idea to know yourself pretty thoroughly and if personality testing will help that, then that's good.

The Keirsey Temperament Sorter gives you wonderful letters to be known by – the ESTJ type or the INFP type.

Knowing ourselves

Whatever method we use to find out more about ourselves is fine just so long as it works and gives us practical and useful and real help. If we are to move on in our life we have to have our dream and be certain that it is attainable – and that means knowing ourselves pretty well. I know, for instance, that I have a real problem seeing things through. Oh, I'm great at generating ideas, sparking off creative brain-storming sessions, but lousy at the detail, the day-to-day, the long-term stuff. It would be extremely foolish for me to take on a dream that required me to be a long-term sort of person. That's why I like writing. Each book requires a lot of ideas and creativity and the actual writing is fun and intensive. And then it is over and I can move on to the next idea.

How about you? What sort are you? Personally I have always found Belbin's types interesting and helpful. Dr Meredith Belbin has spent over twenty years researching the nature of team work and has identified nine distinct team roles:

1 The Plant – original thinkers; they generate new ideas; they offer solutions to problems; they think in radically different ways, laterally, imaginatively.

2 The Resource Investigator – creative; they like to take ideas and run with them; they are extrovert and popular.

3 The Co-ordinator – highly disciplined and controlled; they can focus on objectives; they unify a team.

4 The Shaper – they are very achievement orientated; they like to be challenged and to get results.

5 The Monitor Evaluator – they analyze and balance and weigh; they are calm and detached; they are objective thinkers.

6 The Team Worker – they are supportive and co-operative; they make good diplomats as they want only what is best for the team.

7 The Implementer – they have good organizational skills; they display common sense; they like to get the job done.

8 The Completer – they check details; they tidy up after them; they are painstakingly conscientious.

9 The Specialist – they are dedicated to acquiring a specialized skill; they are extremely professional; they have drive and dedication.

Now these nine types were originally considered in their role as team members. But often I can use them to find out how a person might be happier.

> *I know, for instance, that I have a real problem seeing things through.*

Suppose for instance that Bill wants out of his computer job. He fancies buying a smallholding. At work – his team – he is recognized as a number 2, *the Resource Investigator* – creative; they like to take ideas and run with them; they are extrovert and popular. Fine, but how does this translate into Bill running a smallholding? Is he likely to run into many new ideas? Is a smallholding a good place for an extrovert? Will he be popular (might be if he raises animals and they take to him)? This is not a test.

I think I might advise Bill to think this through a little better. How about you? Can you put your hand on your heart and honestly say you are pretty good at judging who and what you are and how well you will fit with your dream?

Saying goodbye

This section is about communicating and emotions. Leaving a well-paid job to follow your heart has some side effects you may not have considered or encountered.

1 Others around you assume you are failing in some way.

2 You feel you are failing (or running away) in some way.

3 No one else is interested in your dream.

4 You find it hard to say goodbye.

5 You feel that all those years building a career have been wasted.

6 You miss your friends and the social side of work more than you realized you would.

These side effects are different from the normal ones of getting lonely at first, being skint, having to undergo a steep learning curve as you settle into your dream, that sort of thing.

Let's deal with each of these unexpected side effects in turn (although they might now be expected).

1 Others around you assume you are failing in some way

They will throw anything at you as you threaten the security of the entire trap. If you can escape, they must question why they remain accepting the cheese.

2 You feel you are failing (or running away) in some way

If you feel this then maybe you ain't ready to escape yet. Go back and have some more cheese.

3 No one else is interested in your dream

Of course not. See 1. You threaten their security. Your dream is not their escape ticket – it is yours. They are staying, remember? You mustn't frighten the other mice.

4 You find it hard to say goodbye

Of course you do. Now say it and get out. Change is always hard. But it is essential if you are to survive. If you hanker too much to stay then re-read the answer to 2.

5 You feel that all those years building a career have been wasted

No way. You may turn your hand to something completely different but all those years will never be wasted; they are our formative years, your earning money to see the kids through school years, your get-a-mortgage-and-buy-a-house years, your training-for-this-dream years, your eating-cheese years. Look, if you hadn't eaten so much cheese you wouldn't be so ready to quit the trap. You've needed those years to get you to here.

6 You miss your friends and the social side of work more than you realized you would

Yep, it happens. No point denying it. Work gives us a social safety net that is hard to replace. You will be lonely and cold and frightened for a while. But you will also be alive, stretched, challenged, electrified, fired up, creative and, most importantly of all, FREE.

" *If you hadn't eaten so much cheese you wouldn't be so ready to quit the trap.* **"**

You can't fail, only produce results

Following your dream is what this book is all about. It isn't about being 'successful' in traditional terms (cash, possessions – though they may follow). I don't care if your dream is bigger than mine or better or more fulfilling. The title of this book is *I Don't Want Any More Cheese, I Just Want Out Of The Trap*. That's it. It isn't:

I Don't Want Any More Cheese, I Just Want Out Of The Trap And I Want To Build A New Organization That Will Offer Cheese To Others And To Be A Successful Entrepreneur Working Every Hour Under God's Sun Just To Pay For More Mindless Holidays In The Caribbean.

To handle yourself, use your head; to handle others, use your heart.

Donald Laird

part **4**

A dream is an answer to a question we haven't yet learned how to ask.

Fox Mulder

How are you going to do it?

What steps do you need to take to realize your dream? How much money do you need to survive on if you decide to pack it all in and move out of your job? Where are you going to escape to? What price are the houses there? What shape does your dream take? What will you have to do to realize it? Do you need any training? This is the bringing together of all the things you will need to escape but you don't actually escape yet.

The more I want to get something done, the less I call it work.

Richard Bach

OK, let's assume you have your dream. Between dream and reality there is a lovely stage called 'planning'. This stage can last as long as you like. In some cases it lasts indefinitely. In some cases dream and reality never quite meet and planning is the journey, the adventure. I know of one chap, bless his heart, who has spent the last thirty years planning a round-the-world trip in his boat. He knows all the trade winds, all the ocean's currents, the harbours, the charts, the lights, the flags. Trouble is he has never moved from his armchair and lives in central London. Oh yes, another thing, he doesn't have a boat.

But ask him what his dream is and he will tell you all about it and make it sound so realistic, so close, so near that anyone who doesn't know him will believe he's off next week. Well, next month at the very latest. Those of us who know and love him never let on that we know he's never going. Does he know? Oh, I think so, but his planning stage is so valuable to him, so perfect, that he has never yet had to get his feet wet.

❝ *Between dream and reality there is a*
lovely stage called 'planning'. **❞**

So planning is the go-between. It marries dream and reality. If dream is the destination and reality is the journey, then planning is the map.

I am impelled, not to squeak like a grateful and apologetic mouse but to roar like a lion out of pride in my profession.
John Steinbeck

I know of another chap who does indeed have a boat. A fine sailing ship. He keeps it at Falmouth and each year paints it from top to bottom, anti-fouls it against gribble worm – the scourge of the South Seas – and re-varnishes all the lovely old wood. Ask him when he is going and he just smiles and says, 'No'. Ask him why and he points one lazy finger out to the estuary and beyond, to the open sea, and smiles again and says, 'What, go out there, are you mad? That's dangerous. People drown out there'. And he's quite, quite happy to stay where he is, planning his great voyage and never getting beyond having his ship ready to go even if he isn't.

Both men have their dream and their reality. To us they may seem as if they ain't going anywhere. But to themselves they have already arrived. And arrived at a rather wonderful place called 'peace'. Here they have put down anchor and settled into the reality of their dream via their planning. They are happy. They are to be envied. They have achieved nirvana. Envy them – don't ever be tempted to try to stir them up or beat them up for procrastination or laziness. They have their dream. It may not be yours or mine but they are happy. And that, my dear friend, is the answer we are all looking for.

❝ *They are happy. They are to be envied.*

***They have achieved nirvana.* ❞**

Time for a quick story.

There is a man sitting on the river bank fishing. A business executive is passing in his chauffeur-driven limousine. He reacts so badly to the sight of a man sitting so idly wasting his time that he has to stop and harangue the fisherman.

'What the blue blazes do you think you are doing!' he shouts.

'Fishing.'

'But for heaven's sake, don't you think you ought to be doing something more productive?'

'Such as?'

'Well, some work for a start.'

'Why?'

'You could work hard and climb the ladder.'

'Why?'

Because then you'd reach the top, get to be the boss.'

'Why?'

'Well,' explained the business man in an exasperated tone, 'then you get to take time off, do your own thing, be your own man.'

'And what would I do then?'
'For heaven's sake. You could do anything you want. You could take the whole day off and go fishing!'

Research the market

Having a dream is great. Knowing yourself and being emotionally prepared is also great. But if you want to turn dream into reality, you have to know that what you want is attainable and how you are going to attain it. You can divide this knowing into two sections:

- Learning
- Practising

Learning

First and foremost you must learn all you can about what it is you want to do. This may include:

- Enrolling at adult education classes (what used to be called evening classes)
- Asking advice from those already doing whatever it is you want to do
- Studying at home
- Trawling the internet for information
- Reading research such as magazines devoted to your intended activity

Practising

If you are serious and really dedicated you should also be practising for whatever it is you want to do. This can include:

- Getting unpaid work experience in your chosen field
- Doing it part-time
- Doing it as a hobby
- Serving a sort of apprenticeship – working with someone already doing it and getting them to teach you the ropes
- Doing it in a small way so you don't have to throw everything in

Obviously you will know best what your dream is and how you could both learn and practise before actually making the grade full-time. There is, however, a lot to be said for committing yourself 100 per cent. That way you don't have a choice.

❝ There is a lot to be said for

committing yourself 100 per cent. ❞

Planning the job you'll love

If you are at the planning stage then you need to evaluate the job you are going to do and make sure it won't turn out to be a pile of crud like the one you're leaving. There are ten easy points to understand if you are going to be successful in your chosen venture.

1 Know who you are

2 Be who you are

3 Have values

4 Live your values

5 Know your strengths

6 Immerse yourself in your dream

7 Follow your heart

8 Be courageous

9 It's good to talk

10 Have a vision

Know who you are

You've got to know who you are, what you are, how you function, what you think and feel and believe in. There's no point taking on board anyone else's opinion of who you are; you have to know it. Once you know who you are it gives you great strength. It makes you invincible because you become a rock. If, deep down, you are unshakeable in the knowledge that you know who you are and are happy with that, then there ain't much that life can throw at you that can knock you off course.

Just when you think you're winning the rat race, they bring in faster rats!

Unknown

Be who you are

Once you know who you are then being it is easy. Being yourself, being who you are should be as natural as getting out of bed in the mornings, but you'd be surprised how many square pegs there are forcing themselves into round holes – and making themselves very unhappy in the process. Look, if you are a traveller at heart and are staying in one place, you're never going to make your heart zing. Or if you are a stay-at-home type and are constantly on the move, out there meeting new people every day, then deep down you are going to be a pretty unhappy bunny. You have to be who you are or you'll go mad.

Have values

You have to know where you'll draw the line. You have to have values – principles these used to be called. If you are living a lie – being and doing things you don't believe in – then your spirit will wither and you will be unhappy. Have beliefs and stick to them. Refuse to compromise these values no matter what.

Live your values

It doesn't matter to me what your values are but it does matter to you, very much. Your values speak volumes about you to you. Your values give you pride, make you raise your head up above the herd. Living your values doesn't mean preaching them to anyone else or wearing them on your sleeve (no idea exactly what that means, guess it must be an old expression for pinning your religious badge on your sleeve in the 'olden' days). Living your values means not compromising, having a dream and going for it – that's what this book is all about. Basically, living your values means refusing to swallow any more cheese – good for you. Living ethically is good, you get to sleep nights.

" Refuse to compromise these values

no matter what. "

Know your strengths

We looked at finding out exactly what your strengths are in the last section but you have to remember them and measure them against your dream at this planning stage.

I once knew a chap who yearned to open a market stall selling antiques. He knew his stuff pretty good – patina and veneer were words that dripped from his lips all the time – and loved the cut and thrust of selling to the public. He was pretty good at finding stock to sell. He even had the stall and a good pitch marked out. But we all knew his venture was doomed to failure. He hadn't really taken himself into consideration. He had focused on the external tangibles – the stock, the hardware, the customers. He had a fatal flaw. He was absolute crap at early mornings. Now anyone who has ever run a market stall knows you have to get up pretty early to get the best pitches and to get set up before the punters turn up. This chap didn't once look at his strengths (and in this case his weaknesses) – what we might call the intangibles, the internals. If he had done he might have modified his dream a bit and not found life so unbearably awful following his dream. He was lucky because his wife bailed him out by offering to open up the stall while he stayed in bed in exchange for him helping her in her business.

❝ Living ethically is good, you get to sleep nights. ❞

Immerse yourself in your dream

Live it, breathe it, love it, wallow in it, bore those around you with it, be there, build it and it will become stuff. You have to immerse yourself totally mind, body and soul in your dream if you want it to happen. You have to have the focus of an athlete coupled with the vision of an entrepreneur. You have to stay mentally in the special place where you don't question that you will succeed. You have to go to bed clutching your dream and wake up with it every morning.

Follow your heart

Oh, he's going to get all New Age on us. No, I'm not. Even the most dedicated hard-bitten business mogul is following their heart. You don't have to be all wibbly and hippie to follow your heart; all you have to have is a heart, a dream, a vision. Then follow it. It's pretty simple stuff, this isn't rocket science. Do what you love, love what you do. If you aren't loving it – hating the cheese – then get out and do something you do love. That's it.

Be courageous

Worrying about what the neighbours/your mother/your friends will say will keep you in the rut well and truly. You have to have courage to go for your dream. So you're stuck in a boring job in sales and you want to be a folk singer (look, someone has to want to be one for there to be any, OK?), then say so and be proud. It doesn't matter what we think (or how we'll laugh at you), what matters is that you have the courage to follow your heart. Only fearful mice like cheese, the rest of us get out.

It's good to talk

Don't bottle it all up – get it out, talk about it. Talk to anyone who will listen. Seek advice at every possible opportunity. Listen to anyone who has something to tell you about your dream – it may contain a gem, a nugget of info that could get you on the road. Planning isn't just doing stuff on paper. Planning is also gathering information from other people, and you only get to do that by talking to them.

66 *Only fearful mice like cheese, the*

rest of us get out. **99**

Have a vision

Having a dream is all very well but you have to have a vision as well. A dream is what you *want* to do. A vision is a picture of you *doing* it. It's a mistake a lot of people make, which is why they don't get beyond this stage, this planning stage. They have their dream but they never actually visualize themselves in that dream. Thus the dream remains exactly that, a dream. Play with your vision. Each day make that vision a little more real, a little more concrete until, without you realizing it, it has become real all by itself.

Nothing is really work unless you would rather be doing something else.

J.M. Barrie

Networking

God, I hate that word but I can't think of another one. Networking. Yep, that's what you are going to have to do a lot of. I have some friends who, at the time of writing, are seeking to get out of London and move into the countryside down my way. I am aware I am being networked right now. I am being worked to suss out properties for them, check my contacts in the media to see if I might know someone who will be of use to them when they want to work down here, and other simple things like sending them the local paper on a fairly regular basis so they can check out properties. That sort of thing. It's fine. They are dear friends and I don't mind being networked like this. Few people do, even strangers. Bear in mind the fact that most people are mostly very nice most of the time. They are mostly happy to help. Obviously sometimes you might intrude and they'll tell you so in no uncertain terms, but on the whole most people are more than happy to be of help. Especially if you flatter them. No, you don't tell them they are gorgeous or smell nice or have great teeth. Instead subtly infer that you envy their way of life and would like to emulate it yourself.

We all like this sort of flattery because it reinforces our own wonderful image of ourselves as trend setters, clever little beasts who saw a way out of the rat race. Flatter someone for being a cheese refuser and they'll help you no end. Find somebody who's doing what you'd like to do and talk to them!

❝ On the whole most people are more

than happy to be of help. ❞

You are what you think. You are what you go for. You are what you do!

Bob Richards

Going freelance

No matter what you choose to do – apart from staying in the job – you'll end up being a freelance or free agent or just a free spirit in some way. The change from employment to self-sufficiency can be scary. If you get your planning right it should be a lot easier. Once you start working for other people on a freelance basis – and this could be as simple as applying to the local farm for some haymaking in the summer; you're still a freelance haymaker – you have to decide what work you do and how much and when you do it. Making these decisions is very different from going in nine to five and getting your work load assigned to you. The downside is you can't phone in sick or goof off or you'll go bust fast. To be successful you'll have to be:

▶ Organized

▶ Motivated

▶ Experienced

▶ Multi-functional

Let's have a quick look at each of these to give you an idea of what you should be planning at this stage.

Organized

Hey, someone is going to have to take over the function of your PR department, your human resources office, your wages department, your health and safety division, your trade union rep, your canteen, your filing clerk and your boss. Yep, it's going to have to be you. You are going to have to do all these tasks – see Multi-functional below – and the one skill you are really going to need is to be organized. You will have to do the paperwork, the filing, the telephoning, getting the work, doing the work, invoicing and going to the bank and post. If you go off on whims and tangents you'll:

▶ Become exhausted

▶ Get confused

▶ Waste time

▶ Get nothing done

▶ Be ineffective with your time

▶ Forget where you live

You have to be organized. Are you? Come on, be honest. I thought so. Few of us are. So do something about it now. It might be as simple as investing in a decent filing system (or getting someone else to set it up for you) or having a good long hard look at yourself and deciding to pull your socks up. Being disorganized at work and taking the cheese is easy, but doing it when working for yourself just doesn't work.

Motivated

Getting to work when you accept the cheese is made easier for you. If you are late, the boss balls you out. If you goof off, the boss balls you out. If you fail to meet your targets, the boss balls you out. Basically the boss keeps you on your toes and your nose pressed to the grindstone. Tell the boss to stuff the cheese and you lose that motivating force. You have to replace it with yourself. Hey, you're the one who can't get out of bed without ten alarm clocks and an early-morning call from BT. So what are you going to do about motivating yourself?

I know that living close to the edge of the breadline is a fine way of keeping us focused. Yes, I really do know. I live there a lot. I too get up late, wander about in my dressing gown pretending I am thinking. I watch morning TV and spend leisurely hours reading the papers telling myself I will be at my desk by ten every morning. I consider it a major step forward if I'm there by lunchtime. Yep, motivation when you work for yourself can be a bit of a bugger. You're going to have to work on it.

❝ *Living close to the edge of the breadline is a fine way of keeping us focused.* **❞**

Experienced

You gotta know what you are doing. It's as simple as that. No one is going to pick up the pieces for you if you muck up. No one is going to carry the can, take the blame, tell you where you're going wrong, hold your hand or pat you on the back. You have to know what you are going to be doing. If you don't then learn it now while you still have the safety-net of your current employment. Use this working time as planning time – planning your great escape.

Multi-functional

I imagined being a writer meant I sat at a desk and wrote. Hey, it should be so easy. Instead I also have to be:

▶ Receptionist – someone has to answer the phone

▶ Negotiator – someone has to discuss money and terms with publishers

▶ Book-keeper and accountant – someone has to work out whether I'm making a profit or not

▶ Human resources department – I have to pay my National Insurance, tax, insurance, motoring costs, pension payments, etc – no one does it for me any more

▶ Research assistant – no one else is going to trawl the internet for me or go down to the local library to look something up for me

▶ Canteen assistant – I have to get my own lunch, supervise my own tea and coffee breaks, remember to buy the biscuits

▶ IT helpdesk – that includes banging hard on the side of my computer when the hard drive locks up, mending fuses, putting in new toner cartridges, installing new software

▶ Stationery stock controller – someone has to order the paper and envelopes and stamps and paperclips

God, you're going to have to learn multi-functionality big time if you reject the cheese. Wanna back out now? No, of course you don't because the rewards are so high, aren't they? No, they're not. You may well be:

▶ Poorer

▶ More tired

▶ More stressed (in a different way)

▶ Lonelier

▶ More worried

▶ Harder worked

▶ Thinner, leaner and meaner

God, it sounds awful. Why are we doing it? Well, it does have a few advantages:

▶ You aren't answerable to anyone but yourself

▶ You don't have to accept anyone else's cheese

▶ You don't have to be surrounded by toss pots, idiots and slackers

▶ You can work at your own pace

▶ You can feel satisfied and content knowing you've done it all for you

▶ Your heart sings

▶ You are free

Being multi-functional will bring you rich rewards – not money but a feeling of great satisfaction – if you plan well now. If there is any aspect of your new life you don't understand then for heaven's sake spend the working time now learning whatever it is you need to.

Selling yourself and your services

It is easy to think the world will claw a path to our door once we hang out our board and are sitting back comfortably waiting. It ain't gonna happen. You are going to have to get out there and sell – yourself and your service, whatever it is. Is there a market for whatever it is you want to sell? How do you know? What research have you done? Is it enough? Are you bold and confident enough to phone people and sell yourself or do you get all tongue-tied and embarrassed? You'll need to plan what to do now if selling yourself doesn't come easy.

How good are you going to be about setting prices – and negotiating them up or down? My father-in-law has a good story about a young optician asking a senior experienced optician what he should do about pricing his specs. The older, wiser optician explains: 'You hand them their glasses and say "that'll be £50". If they don't flinch you say "for the frames and another £50 for the lenses". If they still don't flinch say "of course that's £50 each lens"'.

I'm not recommending this, but it is always worth bearing in mind that if the customer doesn't flinch, you may have undersold yourself. You are going to have to know:

- How to set prices
- What others in your industry charge
- How much the market can stand
- What you need coming in to survive
- How much you need to earn to make sure you have covered your income tax, running costs, etc
- How long there is between invoicing and getting paid and whether you can survive
- What you are going to do about late payers, bad debts, customers who won't pay because they feel you've let them down (no, I don't believe this will happen to you but I have to mention it in case someone else gets hold of this book)

" You are going to have to get out there

and sell – yourself and your service. "

Start-up planning

OK, so you've planned what sort of prices you can charge, but how much do you need to start up? You're going to have to think about your start-up costs, including:

- Office space/rental
- Furniture
- Equipment
- Transport
- Special clothing
- Staff costs
- Storage
- Advertising
- Registering a company

Look, I'm sure you can think of a million other costs you are going to have to meet to get you started. All I'm saying is be prepared, get planning.

They say that time changes things, but you actually have to change them yourself.

Andy Warhol

Long-term planning

It is a useful exercise to work out where you are going to be in six months, a year, two years, five years. Just getting out is fine. Knowing what you are going to do is fine. But there is the future to think about. You will need to stay ahead of the game, which means knowing which way your particular industry is going and keeping up with innovations and developments. You may need to take some time out for retraining or developing yourself. If you've set your prices, will these remain static? Will you put them up in line with inflation or some other secret code known only to you? You do need a plan for the future as well as your plan for the immediate cheese-rejection stage.

Planning back slapping

How are you going to know when you have succeeded? If, say, in five years you are running a successful business or are head of a charity or working on your fifth novel, you might sit back and pat yourself on the back. But I doubt it. I doubt you will have made it that far. You will have fallen by the wayside long before because you will have lost heart and lost enthusiasm and lost your way. Five years is too long to gauge success. If you don't get rewards you're going to go mad. You need lots of little back slaps along the way. Promise yourself a slap-up meal after you have:

▶ Registered your company

▶ Made your first sale

▶ Employed your first member of staff

- Bought your first computer/set of ladders/set of tools
- Set up your accounting system
- Paid your first bill

And keep rewarding yourself at every opportunity you can. No one else is going to do it for you. No one else has the right to say you are praising yourself too much, too often, too well. You are now the boss. You are also the staff. Say thank you. Pat yourself on the back. Buy yourself lunch. Give yourself half a day off every now and again. Treat yourself to an extra packet of choccy biscuits. Smile at yourself as you start work each day and thank yourself when you finish work each evening.

❝ You need lots of little back slaps along the way. ❞

You can't have everything. Where would you put it?

Steven Wright

Planning your happiness

Take a moment to consider what will make you happy once you have left the trap. What I mean by this is, how are you going to measure your success? You mustn't replace one trap for another. You have to have some yardsticks to measure your progress from entrapment to blissful cheese-free work. It might be getting your first book written/finished/published/selling over 10,000 copies or getting your first contract worth more than £x or successfully setting up your school for yoga in California. Whatever it is you have to have some way of judging that you've succeeded.

This isn't a goal-orientated thing. I'm not saying you have to make it. Hey, you can set the target. It might be just saying no to the cheese. That's fine. You set the targets, not me. I'm not urging you on. I'm not telling you, you have to aim high, aim big. All I'm saying is you need some way of knowing what turns you on, how you can judge that you've achieved your happiness.

It takes a lot of courage to release the familiar and seemingly secure, to embrace the new. But there is no real security in what is no longer meaningful. There is more security in the adventurous and exciting, for in movement there is life, and in change there is power.

Alan Cohen

Of course it might not be a tangible target. Instead you might judge it by saying, 'I'll know I've achieved success when I can start each day by leaping out of bed feeling enthusiastic about what I do instead of crawling out like I've died as I do now'. Or, 'I'll know I'm happy when I can stay in bed all day and not feel guilty'. Hey, do some work on this yourself will you and you decide.

&& Hey, you can set the target. It might be just saying no to the cheese. &&

Planning your health

Leaving cheese behind can generate more stress than staying and eating cheese for ever. You need to plan how you are going to look after you. Things to think about are:

- Eating healthily
- Taking some exercise or doing some sport
- Taking time off
- Not working after 6pm or at weekends
- Taking long and regular holidays
- Taking time off for treats and indulgences
- Spending good time with your partner and/or children
- Having hobbies and other things to do outside of work
- Having friends and socialising
- Belonging to some organizations (no, not the AA, I mean social organizations where you meet like-minded people. No, I'm not giving examples)
- Keeping up some form of religious belief (research in the States has shown that heart attack patients recover quicker and are much less likely to have a recurrent attack if they have a strong religious faith – no, don't ask me why)

There is no such thing as a stress-free life – well, there is, it's called death. If we are alive we are subject to some form of stress. It is what we do with the stress that helps or hinders us.

“ *There is no such thing as a stress-free life.* ”

In the last section we looked at the emotional turmoil that leaving cheese can cause. You will need to do something about the stress. You will need to be positive about it. Obviously not accepting cheese can help enormously, but don't be so naïve that you think all stress will evaporate. It won't, so you do need to have a plan for what you are going to do about it.

Plan time for yourself

This might be as simple as saying 'every Wednesday I shall treat it as early closing and spend the afternoon being nice to me and doing something indulgent and entertaining'. I know you need to work hard and put in long hours, but you also need to be nice to yourself. No one else is going to, so you have to be your own support system.

You could spend a little time now just thinking about how much time you actually spend on yourself. There are seven key areas that need nourishment in our lives if we are to be well-rounded and happy humans. In your planning stage look ahead and see what making the move will do to each and all of these areas:

- ▶ Family
- ▶ Health
- ▶ Money
- ▶ Mental
- ▶ Social
- ▶ Professional
- ▶ Emotional

Family

Will your family be happier? Healthier? Can you get the kids to change schools easily? Have you checked out the schools? Do you have an ageing relative who might need care and you near at hand to look after them in the next few years? Will your partner be able to support you in this new venture? Are they happy with the move/change? These are the sorts of things you should be planning.

Health

Will the move/change be good for your health? If you stay where you are, will you get fat and lazy? How important is your health to you?

Money

You may make less but feel better about it. You may make more. Money is only a tool for getting other things done, but you do have to think about it. You have to think about what your bank balance can stand and how good your savings are and what will happen to your pension. You have to plan your financial position, but it's only one aspect of your new life and shouldn't be the be-all-and-end-all. Money should be only one part of the jigsaw, one slice of the pie, one pawn on the chessboard, one spoke in the wheel (stop me when you've had enough).

Mental

If we process widgets every day of our life, our brain shrivels up and we go all grey and blank and stupid. We all need to be challenged, stimulated, driven, forced to think, used and exercised mentally, confronted, stretched and challenged some more. We need our new life outside of the trap to keep us young and mentally alert and active. Bear it in mind when you are doing your planning.

❝ *We all need to be challenged, stimulated, driven, forced to think.* ❞

Social

We are social animals and need to have friends around us. Packing it all in and going off to some remote place where you know no one and have no friends will cause you a lot of stress, attractive as the idea might be at the time. We need the support friends give us, the cut and thrust of social interaction. We need to be loved and to know that we are loved. Office friends can give us camaraderie, entertainment and the like, but it is rare that they are true friends (OK, I know you might have one or two real friends whom you met through work but on the whole they are ships that pass in the night). Real friends are the ones who are there to help us pick up the pieces when it all goes wrong. They listen to us without judgement and support us when we need them – and it works both ways of course; we are there for them too.

Oh like a bird on the wire, like a drunk in a midnight choir, I have tried in my way to be free.

Leonard Cohen

Professional

What do we mean by this? Why, that old thing pride of course. We have to take pride in what we do. We have to turn out work to a good standard and not let ourselves down. We have to do the very best we can. We have to be professional – deliver on time, be smart and presentable, never over promise and under deliver, speak the truth, be honest, be hard working, be generous in our dealings with others. In general we have to be professional.

Emotional

Try as hard as you like to distance yourself from feelings, you'll find you can't. You have to take into consideration the fact that you are an emotional being. You will have ups and downs, good days and lousy ones. Days when the sun shines and you feel like work and days when it's raining and you feel like crawling back under the covers and staying there for the whole day. You will cry and get angry, be calm and hopeful, have triumphs and setbacks. You will lose heart, gain confidence, seek hope and lack conviction. You will run the whole gamut of emotions from despair to joy.

It makes sense to check out what you think your emotional life is going to be like once you've escaped the trap. Do you see escape as escape or running away? How you see it defines how you begin this great adventure.

❝ You will have ups and downs, good days and lousy ones. ❞

The great escape

If you are planning your great escape it doesn't hurt to see it as a physical escape, a real escape from something such as prison. You would need to have:

▶ A plan
▶ Tools to dig out

- Identity papers in case you get stopped
- A prison guard's uniform
- Money
- Tickets

The plan

Your dream is your plan – this is your way out. You will have something to do. Now make a list of what else you are going to need. Instead of writing down things like false papers and guard's uniforms, try writing down things like:

- Somewhere to live
- A way and means of paying the rent and feeding the kids

That's really about it. The rest will slot into place. I watched one of those wonderful relocation programmes on TV the other evening about a couple relocating to Greece. Basically they just packed up and left for hotter climes. After a couple of months they were back home with their tails firmly between their legs. The reasons? Oh, many and varied. Here's a quick list. I do hope you will never have to make such a list. Adequate planning will make sure you don't.

- They arrived not speaking a single word of Greek
- They had no work permits or documentation
- They had nowhere to live
- They had no jobs to go to

- They had little in the way of savings – and all their money was in sterling and they couldn't work out how to convert it into euros

- They knew nothing of the culture, so the whole idea of something as simple as the siesta came as a shock to them. 'You mean everyone goes to sleep in the middle of the day?'

- They had arrived at the airport with their luggage seriously overweight and thus had to pay penalty charges that were exorbitant to say the least

- They had no insurance, medical or otherwise, and had assumed there would be a National Health Service just like at home

- They had no friends where they were going, not even acquaintances, and would have been entirely thrown back on each other's company all of the time

- They had no idea about local tax affairs and had to employ a local agent to sort out everything for them at quite a cost

- They had no residency papers and again had to employ an agent

- They had no transport, no local licence, probably no idea that they even drove on the right, although perhaps I am being a bit unfair here, maybe this was the one bit they had researched, planned in some way, but somehow I doubt it

- They had a vague idea about starting an internet café but only realized when they got there that most of the local population in the town of their choosing were web illiterate and that all local software was in Greek, which they of course didn't speak or write, let alone run a web site in

They thought it was all going to be hunky-dory (whatever that means) but it was a nightmare (we know what that means). Even a little bit of adequate planning would have saved them lots of money and a lot of stress and hassle.

Saying goodbye to the cheese is easy. Having a decent plan to escape is more difficult. If you don't plan properly, chances are you'll be back begging for cheese within a very short space of time.

Quick recap

To properly escape the trap you need to work out well in advance what it is you are going to do and how you are going to do it. You will need to know:

▶ Where are you going to live?

▶ How are you going to make some money?

▶ Who will be around you to help?

▶ What are the local schools like?

▶ Where are the local shops?

▶ Do you speak the lingo – technical or local language?

▶ Will you fit in or stick out like a sore thumb?

▶ Have you allowed for a seven-point plan of happiness?

▶ Is everyone else on board?

❝ If you don't plan properly, chances are you'll be back begging for cheese within a very short space of time. ❞

Researching your chosen escape route

Look, going it alone is always hard, always tricky. As someone once said, 'If it was easy they'd all be doing it'. Well, they ain't. And they ain't because it's bloody hard work. And a lot will fall by the wayside before reaching the goal because it is so hard. The rewards when you get there are fabulous though, so don't go giving up on me, d'ya hear?

Good. Glad you're still on board. Now look, you've had your dream, had it for years. You've always wanted to ....[5] and now you simply must or you'll burst. You've had enough of the job and want out. Great. Now you must plan how this dream is to be turned into a reality and then you must plan WHAT IS GOING TO HAPPEN THEN. I put that bit in capitals to make you notice it.

---

[5] Please insert your own dream here. Please do this in ballpoint pen so effectively the book is defaced and that means it can't be returned to the publisher which makes it a firm sale which means I collect my 50p for writing it.

I wanted to be a writer. That was my dream. Fine. I did it. Eventually. But I didn't plan what was to happen next. And do you know what? I had to go on being a writer. Every single day I had to be a writer. I have to sit here churning this stuff out. I have to be a writer not once but again and again and again. I have to be a CONTINUOUS writer. And that's the hard bit. That's the bit I hadn't thought about. I have to generate new work, smarm up to new publishers, bang out this stuff five days a week. I had dreamt of being a writer and it had kind of fizzled out after that. What sort of writer? Didn't really know. How many books a year? Didn't know. What sort of living did I think I would be able to earn? Didn't really know. What were my long-term plans? Didn't really know. What's going to happen to me when I am too old, too arthritic to type any more? Don't really know.

Would I change it? No way – that bit I do know. I am happy doing this. I just hadn't realized it would be quite so hard, so time consuming. I guess I figured I would bang out one successful book and then spend the rest of the time appearing on chat shows and being stalked by young starlets. Funny that. Instead I haven't appeared or been stalked. But instead had to keep writing to keep the wolf from the door. (Actually I invited him in and we watch daytime TV together. Well, he's lonely too and finds it hard to get going in the mornings.)

" Got the message now? Yep, you have to

work at it. "

Got the message now? What happens after the dream comes true? Do you all live happily ever after or do you have to work at it? Yep, you have to work at it. Or most of us do anyway. Perhaps you'll be one of the lucky sods who hits the cream right off and can retire straight away. Hey, you might be better off playing the lottery if you're gonna work with those kinds of odds. Better to knuckle down and produce a plan right now.

Things to watch out for

▶ Unrealistic expectations

That's about it. You'll earn less, work less, see fewer clients than you think you will. We all think it's going to be a doddle. We all think it's roses all the way. We all think it's a bowl of cherries. Well, it ain't. It's hard graft. It is also satisfying and rewarding and proud work just so long as we don't set our targets too high. Now we can dream high. But we shouldn't expect too much to begin with. It will rain more where you are going than you think. Be prepared. Carry a brolly.

❝ Now we can dream high. But we shouldn't expect too much to begin with. ❞

Oh, and the other thing to watch out for is nostalgia. Once you've left, the old office routine will start almost immediately to evolve in your mind into something glittery and lovely. Make a journal now of all the shit you've had to take, all the nonsense you've had to put up with. Make a video diary if you like and then when that old nostalgia bug gets you, you can watch your video diary and see how stressed you look and hear yourself moaning on about how shit it is. Don't be fooled by looking back and regretting leaving. It was cheese then and you knew it then. Now you are free, it pays to remember how awful it was. Some people crack eating cheese. Don't let it happen to you. Get out, little mouse, get out now.[6]

[6] I'm putting a footnote here in the hope that it will make my publisher leave this sentence in. They don't want this book to be too subversive. They don't want workers across the land throwing down their tools, casting aside their cheese, and walking out chanting, 'We don't want any more cheese, we just want out of the trap'. They figure it might be bad for the economy or something. I say fiddlesticks to that and if everyone chooses to have a revolution then things will change and change fast. But it won't happen like that. This cheese thing will only get to a few like-minded souls. The rest, not you, are happy to go on taking the cheese. You'll escape.

Last Part

Actions

Self-esteem must be earned! When you dare to dream, dare to follow that dream, dare to suffer through the pain, sacrifice, self-doubts, and friction from the world, you will genuinely impress yourself.
Dr Laura Schlessinger

Taking the first steps

Sometimes to make a dream a reality it requires no more than making a phone call or buying a book or asking someone for some advice. It might not take much, but taking that first step can be enormously difficult. This section explains the importance of doing exactly that though. Yep, this is the section in which you have to start doing things.

I am a great believer in luck, and I find the harder I work, the more I have of it.

Thomas Jefferson (1743–1826)

The chicken moment

So how do you know when it is time to take that first step? What should that first step be? How do you demonstrate to yourself and others that you are serious? Easy. You reach the chicken moment.

I worked with Dougie for several years and I knew that he too had a dream – his own farm. He didn't want anything too big, a sort of smallholding. I wanted to be a writer. Looking back I think everyone I worked with had a dream. We were all there for the money, the cheese, and all longed for escape. One day we came into work and found Dougie had brought in a chicken with him. He had been to an early-morning auction of livestock and couldn't resist this chicken. It was his first step.

66 You have to start doing things. 99

We all then knew:

▶ Dougie was serious

▶ Dougie was leaving us very soon

▶ Dougie was about to realize his dream

▶ Dougie no longer was putting the fear of management in front of his dream, he was now in charge

▶ Chickens and work don't go together

How did we know the last one? Easy, Dougie had to keep the chicken somewhere while we worked so he kept it in his locker. Fine. He gave it lots of breaks and let it walk around a bit, but basically it stayed in his locker. He said it was a chicken and chickens are used to that sort of thing. We all saw nothing wrong with that.

66 One day we came into work and found Dougie had brought in a chicken with him. 99

Dougie's locker was on the third floor so to speak – it had two layers of lockers underneath it. The next shift coming in was not amused to find their stuff newly coated in very runny, very smelly chicken waste. But did Dougie care? Not a bit. He had reached his chicken moment. What will yours be?

You've achieved success in your field when you don't know whether what you're doing is work or play.

Warren Beatty

Our own private chicken moment

For each of us our own private chicken moment comes when we least expect it. For Dougie it was one sunny early morning standing at a livestock auction dreaming his dream of farming in the Cotswolds. Suddenly, on a whim, an impulse, he found his hand shooting up and bidding for a chicken. My own moment also came one early sunny morning. I had been going to work by motorbike[7] for a while and it was exceptionally sunny. The night before I had had a dream about my bike turning over in the air in slow motion but I dismissed this as just a dream.

Getting hit hard

Heading for the city I went to overtake a left-turning lorry (yes, I know, a stupid manoeuvre but I thought it was the left-turning lorry that was going to get me and I was avoiding it) and got hit by a lorry coming out of the left turning that was being shielded by the lorry I was overtaking. I got hit hard as I was just beginning to open the bike up to accelerate away. I came to in the hospital, badly bruised with a shattered collar bone. I couldn't drive for six weeks. I sued the lorry that hit me and got a reasonable amount of compensation, but my employer

---

[7] It was supposed to be a cost-saving exercise – cheaper and quicker than the car for commuting – but in reality I was born to be wild, or so the voice in my head told me.

claimed most of it in lieu of the wages they had paid me for the six weeks sick – it was in my contract that anything I got from a third party for illness or injury could be offset by my employer against wages paid out.

I didn't end up with a lot, but during those six weeks I had plenty of time to think. And what I thought about was, what was I doing risking my life for a job I hated in a place I loathed for a boss I detested? Strong thoughts when you're lying on a sofa in pain and unable to find a comfortable position in which to settle. Yep, I had reached that 'I don't want any more cheese, I just want out of the trap' moment.

" What was I doing risking my life for a job I hated? "

A magic, dream year

I figured that with what was left of the compensation and by cashing in my pension and a bit of savings and if I sold the second car I would have enough to support me for a year. A magic, dream year in which I could do whatever I wanted. I could write my great novel. If it all went wrong I could always get another job at the end of the year, I reasoned.

Adventure isn't hanging on a rope off the side of a mountain. Adventure is an attitude that we must apply to the day-to-day obstacles of life – facing new challenges, seizing new opportunities, testing our resources against the unknown, and in the process, discovering our own unique potential.

John Amatt, Canadian climber

More cheese

When I was better I went into work and handed in my notice. Obviously this was after discussing this with my family, who all backed me 100 per cent, which was reassuring and very supportive and gave me immense confidence that I was doing the right thing. Once I'd handed in my notice I got offered … yep, you've guessed it, more cheese.

Please stay

They, the directors, asked me to stay and wanted to know what it would take for me to withdraw my resignation. I gave them a list:

▶ Instant upgrading to the pay level two above my current one

▶ A company car – this was in the days when they weren't as common as they are now and no one else there had one

▶ An expense account to pay for any out-of-pocket expenses I might incur

▶ Changing my office to a new one which was four times the size and had a better view

▶ Getting rid of my immediate manager and letting me have his job

▶ Working total flexitime and coming and going as and when I saw fit

▶ A computer to be installed at home linked to the mainframe at work so I didn't have to ever go in if I didn't feel like it

- ▶ Not to have to attend any more daft meetings
- ▶ More staff for my department – I asked for another four on top of the four I already had (there was enough work for about four but I fancied asking for more just to see how much cheese was available and how far I could push them)
- ▶ My annual holiday entitlement to be increased from the current one month to six weeks
- ▶ Never to have to work late, overtime, weekends or my birthday
- ▶ To wear whatever I wanted to work

Unreasonable bustards

Look, I'm not joking about any of this. I had a cushy job with lots of cheese and I was pushing them really, really hard to see how much more cheese they would throw at me. They threw the lot except for one condition which they said they simply couldn't fulfil and this allowed me to then leave saying they hadn't been reasonable. Unreasonable bustards.

We know nothing about motivation. All we can do is write books about it.

Peter F. Drucker

Committee room indeed!

Oh, the one condition they wouldn't meet? The bigger office. How intolerable. How petty-minded of them. How mean and penny pinching. They did explain I could have the office next door which was about three times the size of my current one and had a nice enough view and the one I had earmarked was unfortunately already allocated to become a committee room and they couldn't reverse that decision. I walked.

This section is all about making that first step. What was mine? Yes, I handed in my notice and I planned a year off, but what was my first step – that one vital step that says 'here I am with my dream in my hand prepared to make a go of this, prepared to be committed'? Easy. I bought a word processor. I was going to be a writer and this was a tool of my trade. I installed a small study in an unused tiny room in the house and set to work.

❝ Here I am with my dream in my hand

prepared to make a go of this. ❞

The end of my year

What happened, you wonder. Did I make it as a writer? No, of course I didn't. I worked hard that year. Finished my fabulous fantasy trilogy. Passed it out and got it back. At the end of the year I hadn't had a single word published. I was skint but happy. I bowed my head, swallowed my pride (as we all must at times) and went back to work. No, not to the same place, but I did land another cushy job and resolved to try again.

If you have built castles in the air, your work need not be lost. That is where they should be. Now put the foundation under them.

Henry David Thoreau

Head down, nose to the grindstone

And there I stayed for quite a while, head down, nose to the grindstone. Eventually I thought, that's it. I have to get out of the trap again. Cheese doesn't do it for me. But I knew I had blown my chances of selling my writing dream to the family again. Next time I would sell another dream entirely. Look, I was unhappy, I would have sold my granny to get out – and to stay out.

> **❝** *I was unhappy, I would have sold my granny to get out – and to stay out.* **❞**

A journey of a thousand miles must begin with a single step.
Lao-Tzu

Your chicken moment

Now how about you? Have you got that chicken moment yet? What are you going to do to take that first important step? Here's a quick checklist to get your juices going; it isn't comprehensive and I'm sure you can think of others:

▶ Register a business name or limited company

▶ Do some market research

▶ Get a part-time job doing whatever it is you want to do in your dream

▶ If it involves moving, visit the area you intend moving to and check out house prices, register with estate agents, look at local schools

▶ Enrol on a course of study, evening classes, etc

▶ Get your house valued

▶ Buy a chicken – or some other piece of essential equipment (if a chicken can be considered equipment)

▶ Cultivate a friend who already does whatever it is you want to do and find out how watertight your dream is and what the drawbacks are

▶ Have exploratory talks with your financial adviser to see how it will all pan out

In a sense, it doesn't matter what step you take. All that step does is set your heart racing, show you are committed, get your juices flowing, tell the world you are serious. It doesn't matter what you do just so long as you do something.

❝ *It doesn't matter what you do just so long*

as you do something. **❞**

Escape mark two

And me? Did I escape again? Certainly did. I had managed to buy a house during one of those boom things when prices get very silly. What it was worth in London suddenly made a move to the country attainable and easy. It also freed up enough money to take some more time off and do more writing. Again the writing proved disastrous – well, the writing was brilliant, but the publishers weren't playing ball – but I had made the move away from the smoke and smog and was at least getting fresh air and a better view. I had to go on for a few years running a business management consultancy – at least it wasn't eating cheese and it might have been the pinnacle of someone else's dream, but it wasn't mine and although it was a good and successful business, I still yearned for my dream – until eventually I stumbled on the right style of writing for me (you're reading a bit of it) and the right genre and the right publishers.

If what you're working for really matters, you'll give it all you've got.

Nido Qubein

" I finally got so sick of the cheese I could turn my back on it and walk away. "

Now I write all day and advise embryonic managers less and less. I followed my dream. I escaped the trap. I finally got so sick of the cheese I could turn my back on it and walk away. Would I go back? No way, not ever. I would rather sweep streets, pick cotton, clean lavatories than go back to eating cheese.

Summary

Everyone is trying to accomplish something big, not realizing that life is made up of little things.

Frank A. Clark

We have come a long way together through this book and we now get to the summary, the guts, the important bit if you like. Look, the title of this book says it all – **I DON'T WANT ANY MORE CHEESE, I JUST WANT OUT OF THE TRAP**. But there may be a couple more things to say to you if you are ready to listen. I do appreciate that what I have to say may fall on deaf ears – not yours of course but others who may borrow or nick this book off you.

This is a one-to-one, me to you. You are important enough for me to say what I have to say. And what I have to say is that you are important. You are a fabulous, wonderful, unique, worthwhile human being. No, I'm not going to get all New Agey on you, but it does need saying occasionally and in a real way that you have this life and it is here for your pleasure, entertainment, education and edification. Why waste it on cheese when you could be stimulated, stretched, challenged? Why squander it all on cheese when you could live free and brave? Why put up with what is wrong when you could make it right? Sure, you might fail, but then again you might fail at eating cheese – they may decide not to feed you any more and where will you be then? Better to refuse cheese now rather than be cut off from it later. Better to voluntarily turn down the cheese than be forced to some time in the future.

> **&&** *Why put up with what is wrong when*
>
> *you could make it right?* **&&**

The Blues Brothers had a divine mission. So do you. It is to live fully realized and happy. It is to meet obstacles, jump hurdles, solve problems, face challenges, get knocked back, get kicked down, get up again, walk in the sunshine, make friends, be in love, hold hands, take time off, work hard, cry at times, be cold, be alive and be tested. Nowhere does it say you have to eat cheese. You don't have to eat no cheese.

Problems pose challenges and meeting them is part of the fun. Tennis would be a dull game if you took away the net.

Harold Dynamite Payson, boat builder

I worked for a boss once who would walk through the department each morning and ball someone out – anyone, someone at random, it didn't matter who or what they were doing, they got a bollocking. He would then go to his office for half an hour, put his feet up, drink a cup of coffee. Then he would walk through the department again and be as nice as pie to everyone. I asked him the rationale behind his management style. He said it kept 'em on their toes, they never knew where they were with him, they were frightened of him and thus did as they were told and kept their heads down.

I worked with another chap who once asked me why I had so many children, wasn't it just a lot of hard work? Sure, I said, but occasionally you get the little arms around your neck at bedtime and the 'I love you Daddy'. He looked at me for a long time and then said, 'Get a grip, Rich, get a grip'. He was tough and clean and neat and I was scruffy and tired and soppy.

Sometimes we need to adjust our management style. Sometimes we have to be soppy. Sometimes we have to be kids again and chase a dream. Being grown up is great. We get to have sex, drive cars, stay up late and play with our toys for as long as we want. But we also get responsibility. Responsibility to others, to ourselves, to our community, to our society and to our planet. We have a responsibility to put something back. To not always take but to give as well. We have to be bold and adventurous and foolhardy. We have to be an example to others and we don't do that by buying into the whole cheese thing.

66 We have a responsibility to put something back. To not always take but to give as well. 99

I hear you might say, 'But what would happen to society if we all walked out? Where would we be if we all refused the cheese? Wouldn't the whole thing collapse like a house of cards?'

I still feel like I gotta prove something. There are a lot of people hoping I fail. But I like that. I need to be hated.

Howard Stern

I have no idea what would happen. But I would love to try it and see. I would think it's got to be better if it all did collapse rather than we all went on living grey, dreary lives of quiet desperation.

If you have had enough cheese and long to escape the trap, you have to follow a logical process to make good your exit. There is a step-by-step process to go through.

▶ Have a dream
▶ Know what you want
▶ Talk to others
▶ Create a plan
▶ Take the first step
▶ Wave goodbye

Have a dream

This is a private thing. Don't allow anyone to shoot your dream down in flames. They can offer advice, give you guidance, help you, support you, nourish and nurture you, but they can't piss on your fireworks. That is bad manners. That is forbidden. You hold on to your dream no matter what because there will always be someone somewhere who will laugh at you, hate you for having such a dangerous thing as a dream without a licence, a permit, a cage for it. They are jealous because they don't have a dream. They will seek to kill your dream so you can be like them, cold and grey and dead. They will do anything to persuade you that having a dream – especially one as liberating as yours – is a terrible thing and you are being irresponsible, subversive, seditious, revolutionary, rebellious and anti-everything. Better to let your dream die now and conform, be like them, sell out, buy into, eat cheese.

❝ Don't allow anyone to shoot your dream down in flames. ❞

Don't listen to them. You have your dream and hold it close, feed it, love it, allow it to grow, to come to fruition, blossom, burst forth. Have heroes who had similar dreams. Watch what they did. Be inspired by them. Read their quotes and learn them. Work on your dream every day of your life and never lose sight of it. Go to sleep thinking about it. Wake up in the morning and think about it. Read about it. Talk about it. Breathe, sleep, eat and drink your dream.

The most important thing about motivation is goal setting. You should always have a goal.

Francie Larrieu Smith

❝ Breathe, sleep, eat and drink your dream. ❞

Know what you want

What do we want? We want out. When do we want it? Now! Do we? Have we the courage to take our dream and turn it into reality? Yes, yes, yes. Knowing what you want is taking your dream and writing an objective, building the foundations under the castle in the sky, dotting the Ts and crossing the Is. Knowing what you want is picturing yourself in that dream, seeing the flaws and putting them right before you embark on your perilous and precious journey.

> **Knowing what you want is about**
> **knowing also what you don't want.**

Knowing what you want is about knowing also what you don't want. You don't want to be bossed around, made to feel small, be humiliated, condescended to, put down, enslaved, taken advantage of, used or abused. You want to feel strong and brave and free and proud and honourable and wanted and needed and loved and useful and worthwhile and important. You won't get any of that eating cheese.

Knowing what you want means understanding what makes you tick, what sort of a human being you are and thus where you will be happy, what you will be happiest doing, where to live, what to think and feel and believe. Knowing what you want means knowing what works for you. It might be eating cheese, wallowing, being lazy, not knowing what you want. All of these are fine. There is no pressure, no judgement. Just so long as you are happy then it's fine. As soon as you aren't happy not knowing then you will know what it might be that will make you happy.

This time like all times is a very good one if we but know what to do with it.

Ralph Waldo Emerson

Talk to others

When you have a dream and know what you want, talking to others will lay the foundations that will allow that dream to happen. Bottling it all up won't progress you one step. Talking will allow that dream to happen. When I say talk to others I mean your loved ones, your advisers, your friends, your supporters, those on your side. I don't mean the detractors, the piss takers, the dull, the uninformed, the jealous bastards who would think nothing of stamping on your dream because they feel so shabby, so lost, so hollow inside that they can't bear the thought of anyone escaping the hell they feel best in.

❝ *Bottling it all up won't progress you one step.* ❞

Talk to your partner first. Share your dream with them. Allow them to pull it apart with love and show you the flaws and the mistakes. They will do this because they love you and can be a little more objective than you can. In an ideal world they will have the same dream. Together you can move mountains, change the world, build a reality that is so strong it will make you both supremely happy.

If you don't talk to your loved ones, how will you know what they want? How will you find out what their dream is? How will you discover how compatible your dreams are?

❝ *If you don't talk to your loved ones,*
***how will you know what they want?* ❞**

If we talk we get feedback, new ideas, support, brainstorming, reactions, comments, opinions, views, improvements, pointers and responses. If we don't talk all we get is silence.

Create a plan

To turn a dream into a reality you have to have a plan. This plan is your map, your route to actuality. Without a plan you will flounder, wander about a lot, get lost, lose sight of your goal, fall into the quicksand, get diverted. With a plan you can find your way, follow a series of steps, have some guidelines and generally be able to get back on track easily when you stray. A plan gives you direction and stability.

66 Without a plan you will flounder, lose

sight of your goal. 99

But what is a plan? It is a series of steps you need to take to realize your dream. It might be as simple as 'buy a boat, leave job, sail away'. Or it might be a lot more complex, involving starting a business, buying stock, registering a name, learning a craft or skill, employing people, finding premises, launching a product, and on and on and on.

Nothing is as real as a dream. The world can change around you, but your dream will not. Responsibilities need not erase it. Duties need not obscure it. Because the dream is within you, no one can take it away.

Tom Clancy

You need to have your plan tested to destruction by bank managers, accountants, solicitors, doctors, teachers, whoever. Choose professional people who have no vested interest in approving of a dream. They will tear it all to shreds. Good. They aren't trying to stop you. They are trying to help you but in their own dry way. If you want your plan rubber stamped with approval, show it to me and I'll OK it. I'll OK anything. If you want sensible, practical, dry advice, show it to your bank manager. These are the two extremes. Obviously if you are a bank manager I take back everything I've said. No, seriously, if you are a bank manager, show your plan to another bank manager, not to yourself.

❝ A plan gives you direction and stability. ❞

If the professionals OK your plan then you've got a winner. If they pooh-pooh it, go back to the drawing board and start again. They aren't pooh-poohing your dream, only your way of realizing it this time. Keep the dream, abandon the plan.

Get a new plan, Stan, but set yourself free.
50 Ways to Leave Your Lover, pop song

Don't do anything until your plan is watertight, foolproof, bombproof, idiotproof. When it is you are ready to move on to the next step. Before you go, accept that having a perfect plan doesn't mean it can't fail. There is more Horatio, etc etc.

Don't ever let anyone steal your dreams.
Dexter Yager

Take the first step

People are often surprised by how often alternative medicine seems to work, to effect cures, despite the fact that little of it can be 'proved' by conventional means. How can it be that homeopathy – using untraceable trace elements in water – works? I think, and here I am open to criticism I know, that it works because the ill person made their first step towards good health themselves. I think in a sense it doesn't matter what you do as long as you do something. Once you make that first step things happen because you have embraced change.

" Once you make that first step

things happen because

you have embraced change. "

Getting out of the trap is pretty much the same. Doing something gets the ball rolling and thus you have opened yourself up to change, to the forces of the universe which effect change.

If you do nothing, nothing will happen. If you do something – and it can be a little symbolic act that marks you out as a doer and not just a talker – things can happen. If you do nothing, you have not taken the first step towards commitment to your dream.

" If you do nothing, you have not

taken the first step towards

commitment to your dream. "

In 1995 I climbed to the summit of Mt. Shasta. I'll never forget how I felt as I stood atop that majestic 14,162ft peak. I looked beyond the metal crampons strapped to my hard-shelled boots, and was awed by the expansive views and the realization of what I had just accomplished. Cold and tired, yet completely euphoric, I experienced in that moment an amazing sense of fulfilment. I believe it's a feeling that only comes from pursuing a dream, taking action, overcoming challenges, and finally achieving success.

Michelle Schubnel, life and business coach

Wave goodbye

Once you have made that first step you'll be ready to wave goodbye. And that's a goodbye to whatever you want to wave to. It might be the job. It might be the old you. It might be anything you want. I think life is far too short to put up with crap in it. If it's wrong, get rid of it. If it ceases to satisfy you, dump it. If it no longer sparks your motor, then wave goodbye. But do bear in mind that this doesn't mean reckless disposable relationships. Relationships need work and time and commitment. I'm talking dreams here. Dreams and goals and plans. They can be dumped fast. People can't – they need to be treated kindly. A dream can be replaced easily; a friend or companion or partner or lover can't.

Somehow I can't believe that there are any heights that can't be scaled by a man who knows the secrets of making dreams come true. This special secret, it seems to me, can be summarized in four Cs ... They are curiosity, confidence, courage, and constancy, and the greatest of all is confidence. When you believe in a thing, believe in it all the way, implicitly and unquestionably.

Walt Disney

I think it's time for us to wave goodbye. I have enjoyed this journey with you and hope you will bear in mind the four points:

▶ Dream

▶ Talk

▶ Plan

▶ Do

Easy. Now all you have to do is do.

Go for it, run little mouse, run, escape, be happy.

Richard Templar, writer